A Sense of Place:

An Anthology of
Cape Women Writers

◆

Edited by Anne Garton

SHANK PAINTER PUBLISHING • CAPE COD • MASSACHUSETTS

A Sense of Place

EDITED BY ANNE GARTON

Book Design by Gillian Drake
Cover Photographs by Gillian Drake
This book was set in Adobe Garamond typeface.

Published January 2003 by

SHANK PAINTER PUBLISHING
P. O. Box 720
North Eastham, MA 02651
(508) 255-5084

ISBN: 1-888959-35-5

PRINTED IN THE UNITED STATES OF AMERICA

We are grateful for the support for this anthology provided by the following generous individuals and organizations:

PATRONS
Arts Foundation of Cape Cod *
Barnstable Cultural Council*
Cape Cod Photo Workshops
Charles Sumner Bird Foundation
Chatham Cultural Council*
Eastham Cultural Council
Lois Grayson, West Orange, NJ
Hermes Foundation, Philadelphia, PA
Living Arts Foundation, Truro, MA
Mashpee Cultural Council*
Sandwich Cultural Council*

DONORS
CCBT Financial Companies
Younghee and Arthur Geltzer, Providence, RI
Jack L. Harris, M.D., Harwich Port, MA
Harwich Cultural Council*
Jane J. Lea, Truro, MA
Stephen G. Spear, East Dennis, MA
Truro Cultural Council*
Wellfleet Cultural Council*

SUPPORTERS
Dorothy Cook, Provincetown, MA
Doris Chatterton, Harwich Port, MA
Carol Green, Truro, MA
Wendy Levine, Truro, MA
Anita Mewherter, Orleans, MA
Pamela Chatterton Purdy, Harwich Port, MA
Ronald W. Swanson, Forestdale, MA
The Family of Nancy Dingman Watson

CONTRIBUTORS
Edward & Patricia Balicki, Harwich Port, MA
Susan Parker Brauner, Harwich Port, MA
Nancie Godwin, Brewster, MA
Louis Postel, Cambridge, MA
Judith Richland & Kevin Shea, Newton, MA
Thelma Turner, Harwich Port, MA

MASSACHUSETTS CULTURAL COUNCIL

*THIS PROGRAM IS SUPPORTED IN PART BY GRANTS FROM THE ABOVE-NOTED CULTURAL COUNCILS,
LOCAL AGENCIES SUPPORTED BY THE MASSACHUSETTS CULTURAL COUNCIL, A STATE AGENCY SUPPORTING THE ARTS,
HUMANITIES AND SCIENCES WHICH ALSO RECEIVES SUPPORT FROM THE NATIONAL ENDOWMENT FOR THE ARTS.

DEDICATION

This book is dedicated to the generous individuals
and funding agencies who made
publication of this anthology possible,
and to the imagination of women writing everywhere,
especially those who share their stories with us here.

Contents

III. ON LOVE AND OTHER TIES THAT BIND

IV. PASSAGES AND TRANSFORMATIONS

V. SECRETS AND SILENCES

IN MEMORIAM

Foreword

THE IDEA FOR AN ANTHOLOGY of work by Cape women writers evolved out of *CapeWomen* magazine's annual fiction and poetry contest. The abundance of creative writing that was sent to us, from lyrical poetry to raw memoirs, from humorous essays to flights of fancy, was overwhelming. Since we can publish only a small number of these stories and poems in the pages of the magazine, we decided to produce an anthology which would create an artistic reflection of living as a woman on Cape Cod. Our goal was to publish work by women from every region of the Cape, from all walks of life, and of all ages, and to provide them with the audience they deserve.

To encourage writers to send in their work, we posted announcements of the forthcoming anthology in libraries and other venues around the Cape, and placed ads in local publications, including *CapeWomen* magazine. We sent out brochures and contacted local artists for illustrations for the book. Choosing which work to include was difficult. We decided to limit the selection to 50 writers, representing a broad cross-section of the submissions we received. We were aware that those not included in this first anthology may be disappointed; however, we have announced our intention to create a literary press with the purpose of publishing more books of fiction and poetry such as this one. We hope all women writers living on and inspired by the Cape will continue to send us their work for future publications.

—GILLIAN DRAKE, PUBLISHER

Introduction

CREATING AN ANTHOLOGY is a long and ultimately humbling process. As letters went out and notices were posted, as the stories, poems and essays tumbled in, as I read them and re-read them and wrote their authors, I was astonished not only at the quality of the work that came across my desk but also at each contributor's willingness to share her particular story. They are mostly shadow writers, these women. Many of them are unpublished. Seldom have they found an audience they deserve. That's the humbling part. They're good.

It was clear I would have to impose a structure upon the large number of manuscripts I received. I wanted the sections in this book to have some connective tissue that would run all the way through it. I began to see common patterns and themes emerge and then slide into focus so that, eventually, the chapters formed themselves into a kind of logical configuration. Eventually the stories, poems and essays elbowed into place, asserting their main point, refusing to be ignored. Thus the anthology, in a sense, created itself.

Our "working" title, *A Sense of Place,* became our "fixed" title and the more I thought about the Cape as "place" the more I began to realize how central to the imagination it had become for our writers. We chose this title for our anthology because our contributors seemed to have the exact same feeling about the Cape as we did. In his book, *Primal Place,* Robert Finch writes about a landscape "whose essential character lies in [its] penetrating interface with the sea." I thought how the sea and landscape merging into each other is "primal" in a way women understand at a very deep level. I believe that something like that actually happens. And Finch writes "in order to belong to a land rather than merely to own and occupy it, we . . . must risk going out and being fundamentally changed [by it]." All of this sounds true to me. I became convinced that the sections I created for this anthology all emerge out of a deep understanding of what it is to live and work and be inspired by something like Finch's "primal place."

I began to examine how and in what ways we become native to our place. Not surprisingly, I decided that the whole process is entirely subjective, that every individual walks at her own pace down her own path becoming native in her own fashion. That said, I concluded that all the writers in this anthology are in the right place at the right time to do the bidding of their imagination. They may not live here year-round, they may be seasonal visitors, touching down lightly where someday they hope to land firmly, but they know where their place is, and it's here. I believe that becoming native to this place means falling into harmony with its rhythms, its passages and transitions, its habits and its narratives. And so it is in this spirit that I have collected the essays and poems and stories and organized them in such a way that they give voice to *A Sense of Place*.

The themes and categories that emerged began to reflect how a cultivated sense of place contributes to patterns of risk and change. Permanence is not among my chapter headings. The Cape is a shape-shifter and every woman tuned into the nature of this peninsula knows it deep in the bone. A woman's life is always transitional. She knows that nothing in life is ever permanent, that all of her life is relational. She knows that it is in her nature to be conscious of rhythm and flux. And she is comfortable with that knowledge. She is naturally suited to this environment, for the Cape is not a place of long and stubborn taproots. Flexibility, tolerance, relationship. And so my sections reflect that fluidity, melting into each other as the landscape merges with the sea, recapitulating themselves over and over, like waves.

This is not to say that these writers do not cherish the old values and the old ways. Most of them do, but not without a few hard-nosed reservations. Built into their sense of place is the instinct for survival and an obdurate belief in their ability to locate one's true self and to encourage its need for expression. And so, I open our anthology with the title chapter, "A Sense of Place." It sets a tone of commitment and inspiration lodged within flexibility and change. In her poem "Insomnia," June Beisch asks the essential question . . . "What can we do here but be ourselves?"

Everything builds from a sense of place. Now we can explore themes that every woman seeks out like a sore tooth. In the next chapter, "The Making of Generations," the theme of Elizabeth Goldberg's poem "Gathering Fruit," we begin to look at how relational and generational we are, how vulnerable to the fates of our birth families. Women write about their mothers and their sons and daughters and their grandmothers. Our roots are sunk into the history of generations, not in the shifting sands of Cape Cod, as snug and safe as it makes us feel sometimes. Women are intrigued by their multiple roles within a family and are relentless about it. We turn it over like a pretty shell and we look at it from every angle. In this section we are "Growing Up" and "Gathering Fruit."

And so out of our sense of place, out of our roles as mothers and daughters, some of our contributors begin to explore the confounding nature of love, "The Ties That Bind." Many, *many* woman write about love. Women *love* love. But they are more realistic about it than one might expect. They know it's not for free. They know love *binds* us to our partners, to our children, and as we read, even to our homes, sometimes in ways that are perverse and unfortunate. If we love, we are *not* free. Like anything, love has its dark side, and in this chapter we explore that too, such as the dangerous love in Pamela Purdy's story, "Sister Sally Loved to Death."

By the time we reach the next section, "Passages and Transformations," we know what inspires women to write and what they choose to write about. This section begins appropriately with Anne LeClaire's trenchant essay about change. She writes how change, being "the only constant," often overtakes her. Nothing is static, she says, all is wrapped up in loss and transformation. Her heart, she writes, "is confused and full with the extremes of life." When we love, we must deal with loss and some of us are better at it than others. Age, too, figures in this section importantly. The demographics of the Cape show us that we live in an ageing population and along with our ageing comes a vulnerability that makes us shake in our boots. This is a chapter about death and about acceptance of the ravages and passages of time. In this section, also, are the voices of youth and invincibility. Passages and Transformations.

The chapter, "Secrets and Silences," created itself out of a kind of urgency. Women writing on Cape Cod, like women everywhere, have shrouded their lives in secrets. This chapter gathers up the writings of women who are speaking after a long silence. Women are secretive about many things and their silence is often broken at great cost. There are countless ways a woman is silenced but the lessons are all the same. Shame is a silencer, as in Candace Perry's "Life Drawing." Ambition is a silencer. Teachers are silencers and so are mentors and other such authority figures. In arranging this chapter I am struck by the varieties of ways that women cling to their secrets, and by how their secret ambitions, in many cases, have silenced them.

Finally, I have included a section, "In Memoriam." It will speak for itself, loudly, in the haunting voices of those who have recently left us and who still claim, urgently, to be heard.

— ANNE GARTON, EASTHAM, MA, OCTOBER 2002

I

A Sense of Place

Living and Writing Like a Cape Cod Woman

BY ANNE GARTON

THE CAPE IS THE BEST PLACE I HAVE EVER BEEN. I am a better woman for being here. But assigning identity to place is a complicated thing, and linking it to gender is even trickier. My identity as a "Cape" woman is just one of a whole string of identities. Yet it is the true one. It means I am utterly unable to live for long anywhere else. It means my space on this great dune is my own personal geography. I learned how to cope with solitude here. I think I must be sacrificing something for all of this beauty, but I'm not sure what it is. I seem, happily, to have stumbled on a delicious kind of freedom, the chance to re-create, re-invent myself, over and over. I am still learning the importance of this. The Cape is a commodious and generous place for women.

History tells me this is true. Cape women re-invent themselves as often as they need to, and so does the Cape itself. The Cape is a roguish shape-shifter. It promises change because change is what it does best. It's not a fixed point on the horizon. It transforms itself, too easily, under the twin pressures of nature and humanity. The Cape breathes with possibilities. It offers itself to the artist in everywoman. An elusive seducer. A charming friend, a believer in women's adaptability.

In the early days, Cape men kept their eyes on the horizon. They hunted. They fished. They moved about a great deal, some of them far away. Many of them didn't come back, not for years, not for ever. But Cape women would fix their gaze on the Cape's shifting center. They focused on dailiness. If the dailiness changed, then they would change. They understood the Cape in its intimacies. They were the beachcombers, the field foragers, garden makers, and sheep herders. They were the teachers and healers, the choir and the choirmaster, the mothers and occasionally the fathers. They molded the curving backbone of Cape Cod out of their love and labor. And so I consider them when I think about what it means to be a Cape woman. They have much to teach me.

But my best teachers, dozens of them, haunt the walls of my two-hundred-year-old home. I believe I inherited this house and the land around it from the women who took care of it for so long, longer than there are records, longer than anyone can say for sure. They bequeathed it to me as if I were their own true daughter. Their lessons come to me in whispers and I listen best in the evening quiet or when I am deep in a mindless task.

One of them tells the story of the beginning. A fisherman built this house on the shifting sands of Billingsgate Island. It is a modest but greatly loved house. And so when the currents of Cape Cod Bay slowly dissolve that unfortunate spit of land, the woman in our house naturally considers it too precious to lose, and prepares to move it. It is loaded onto a barge and then floated across the bay like a bloated whale.

I picture that great house-moving adventure through her eyes. I sense she is deeply apprehensive, not only about this monstrous move but about the future she is inching towards. Her rescued home soon sits on a slight rise in the middle of a vast farmstead, and this will change her forever. The sea has gobbled up her island and her whole experience. The Cape has shifted its parameters. All she knows now are asparagus and turnips. In due time, she adapts. She teaches me an important lesson; that to be a true Cape woman, you must be a bit of a shape-shifter yourself.

She is a sharp woman, this ancestor of mine, and the ones who follow, and she sees the Cape buckle under the pressures of too much farming, too much logging, too many sheep, too little conservation. Soon the farm is depleted, pared down to scrubby pine and sand. It is not possible to grow asparagus and turnips in sand. But now she knows how to navigate change. She looks around. She takes account of the hundreds of summer people pouring onto the Cape by boat and train. They come for religious awakenings, for family reunions, for such pleasures as summer brings, and so she re-invents herself again. Turning the upstairs into a rabbit warren of rooms, she is innkeeper, cook, chamber maid and laundress. Up and down the street, in house after house, Cape Cod women do the same thing.

And as the tourist trade blooms, additions to the house sprout in true New England fashion. Kitchens and bathrooms proliferate. Porches rupture ancient walls, front and back. Cabins spring up on the back meadow, beds of iris flag down the tourists who motor along the new highway. At the end of the season, the Cape woman in my house says good-bye to the strangers and retreats to the warmth of this house and the pleasures of a solitary winter. This is how she teaches me solitude.

Suddenly, and she doesn't exactly know how, the land is subdivided and sold again. The cottages are strung together into a pizzeria and donut shop facing east on Route 6. The Cape woman in my house blooms as a chef and waitress, a maker of donuts and pizza. A new alley slices between the old house and next door, joining the busy highway to the once quiet back road. And then she moves south to Florida, leaving the house to winter alone. By the time I take my turn the old place is semi-abandoned, a sad anomaly. The land has shrunk to half an acre of lilacs and roses, dead cedars and privet.

But the ghosts of my teachers are still in residence and the lessons come hard and fast. In my garden I uncover the shards of my female ancestry: mysterious parts to an ancient toaster, medicine bottles, an exquisite perfume stopper, kitchen scrapers, countless jars of every color and size, shell middens and canning supplies, clamming baskets and bicycle parts. Lessons come while sweeping the sand across these ancient floorboards, watching most of it drift down to the cellar hole. They come from the layers of milk paint and wallpaper in the bedrooms, from rare herbs poking through tangled roses, from old calendars and advertisements carefully pasted onto pantry doors. Someone tells me the saddest story about a small child who died in the bedroom under the eaves. And they have felt, on occasion, the ghost of a woman, her mother, in the tick of an unnatural breeze, a sudden chill in midsummer.

But I have never sensed the presence of this mother's ghost. Not in that way. Instead I feel a happy kinship with that mother's mother, that mother, that child, this house, this land, those beaches over the highway. My ghosts are the women who staged the Thanksgivings and Christmases and birthdays in this house, year after year, two hundred and fifty of them.

My rocking chair burnishes the same tread on our porch. The wild cats in the barn, the skunks under the ell, the cardinals who descend to my feeders, the doves in the spring, the generations of birds and animal life who shelter here, I am convinced, have been shared by all of us.

I think about our Cape woman's unwritten history now as our Realtor hammers the "For Sale" sign into the front garden of this anachronistic old house. It sits uncomfortably in the middle of a busy, year-round commercial zone. I think it has outlived its time as a place for women. We try to talk over the din of delivery trucks and traffic on Route 6. I wince as a fire engine screams past. It no longer feels right here.

The Cape women, my teachers who loved this house, no longer haunt it. This could be a dentist's office, my Realtor says, or an antique dealer's. I nod in agreement. It could. Or, she adds, ominously, maybe the land is more valuable by itself, and I look stricken. But then I remember. I am a shape-shifter, now. Adaptable. I've been well-taught. The Cape is a commodious and generous place for women.

MARIAN ROTH, PINHOLE PHOTOGRAPH

Insomnia

BY JUNE BEISCH

Alone on the Cape in a new year
and all night long the thundering sea
invades our dreams, the stars anchor down
on these black nights like fate.

What can we do here but be ourselves?
The sea answers only to its own turbulence,
the moon rocks in its chamber,
the days flatten out into oblivion.

At night, you pace the living room awake,
the stifling cry of some night wandering loon
is company. I want to share your loneliness,
but loneliness cannot be shared.

I think of how I once had prayed
for a life of the finest intensity.
But what is poetry if not life
at its finest intensity?

Washashore

BY JAMIA KELLY

I came here broken,
like a spring wound
far beyond its bearing.

The gentle rhythms
of the tides
surge high
and low,
the tide of days
and years falling
from a peak of frenzy
to the rank exposure
of the mossy bottom,
secretly alive
with armored burrowers,
scurrying to hide
beneath the sand.

Unnoticed,
slowly, once again
the seeping, creeping
dancing waves of sparkling joy
have filled the empty bowl of bay
and lifted me ashore
renewed,
newborn,
hidden in the wrack
of sea washed bones
and rotting grass.

Dune Haven

BY RUTH LITTLEFIELD

Unknown Woman Found in the Dunes, July 26, 1974
Briefly Exhumed, March 23, 2000

She sought the
serenity
of her
self-proclaimed
dune.
Her dune awaited
manifesting a
welcome.
She was of a
different age.
Her arrival
in time
premature.
In the dunes
she found
contentment
comfort
liberation
from life,
her troubled mind
at peace.
Kneeling on
warm sand,
her flowing
chestnut brown hair
blowing with
abandonment,
her bronzed face
tilted toward
the sun.

Glistening tears
upon her face.
fell.
Cleansing her
being
out of the
peacefulness.
Tempestuous
summer storm.
An overcoat of
ebony
enveloped all.
Powerful winds
blowing
churning
grains of sand.
Uprooted dancing
dune grass
seeking refuge
in the plaiting
of her hair.
Each grain of
dune sand
caressing her
silently, lovingly,
cloaking her
anguished body,
mesmerized
by the
phantoms
of the
dunes.
Infinity.

Enid's Wall

BY JENNIFER GOSTIN

THIS IS THE STORY OF SWEET ENID OF EASTHAM, who came to a dreadful end through love. Not of man, woman, child, nor of any breathing thing, for that matter. Love of a place is what did poor Enid in. The trouble was that the object of her passion was the Outer Cape, a setting that's real and unreal at once, that's grit-cold windy and plain as baked codfish, and at the same time misted with tales and legends. The light's justly famous, but there's fog, too, and plenty of it.

Enid bought the house across from mine, down this lumpy road off another lumpy road that darts off Route 6 just where no sane person would expect a road to be. Mine's a nineteenth century farmhouse, much modernized and too big for me now, but home. Hers is a three-quarter cape, built in the twenties, little altered. We're tucked back in the pitch pine and scrub oak woods. Of the ten houses on the street, only three others are lived in year round, all by busy families with jobs and kids in school.

So the day after the Atlas truck drove away, I went over to welcome her to the neighborhood. She beamed at the covered dish I'd brought, though she seemed slightly disappointed when I told her it was chili. I learned later that she regarded New England cuisine with deep veneration, and was probably hoping for Indian pudding or stuffed quahogs, something more geographically appropriate.

You couldn't tell her age by looking at her. She was retired, so I assumed her to be over sixty-five, but then some folks get encouraged to move along early. And some folks never looked young, even when they were. Enid was like that, sharp-boned, mottled, and toothy. She'd humped up her long graying hair with antique clips into a sort of topknot.

That first day, she sat on the floor and unpacked while we chatted. Books by the boxload—turns out she was born and bred in the suburbs of Washington DC, where she taught high school English most of her life. *All* her life, she said, she'd wanted to live on Cape Cod. She'd had two husbands, one divorce, one death, no children. Two honeymoons, one in Hyannis and one in Truro, and an occasional weeklong trip up here when she could afford it. With each visit, she found it harder to pull away.

Her experiences hadn't affected her romantic outlook, I thought, watching her start on a carton of clothes. She unfolded and hung a flowery array of Laura Ashley and the like, yards of dainty prints, crisp cotton, and eyelet.

"And now here I am," she said, taking in her surroundings with almost religious awe. "To stay."

I told her we had some things in common. I'd lost my husband, too, three years after we moved here from Waltham. The house had been in my family since the fifties, when my parents bought it for clan gatherings. I'd inherited it in the seventies, and Geoff and I came full time in '92, letting him enjoy a few years of retirement. Now there was just me.

"So you have real roots here!" Enid looked at me like I'd fished off the deck of the

Mayflower.

I couldn't help but laugh. "You're not a native unless your parents were born on Cape, at the very least. The more times your name turns up on old tombstones, the better. But I've been around long enough to help you out if you need to find a dentist or a hairdresser. And I know a great plumber."

Folks around here can be standoffish and wave their family histories around like so many flags, but when you're really down and out, they're solid as Doane Rock. I learned that when Geoff died, and people whose names matched the ones on street signs and historical placards mowed my lawn and plowed my driveway. Some whose kin had hauled lobsters out of the bay for five generations brought me warm dinner plates wrapped in tinfoil and gave me a reason to pick up my mail when I felt too sad to get out of bed.

But I got used to the term "washashore" years ago and advised her to do the same.

"Oh, this *is* my true home. I've always known it. Listen to this . . . ." She began to recite. 'Sometimes a man hits upon a place to which he mysteriously feels that he belongs. Here is the home he sought, and he will settle amid scenes that he has never seen before . . . . Here at last he finds rest.'"

Enid offered me a beatific smile. "That's from Somerset Maugham. Don't you think it's true? You can substitute the feminine pronoun, of course," she added.

I smiled back. It was a pretty sentiment, and maybe it belied those Cape Cod Tunnel stickers and back-bumper ropes and all the other tricks meant to make newcomers feel like strangers.

But Enid wasn't finished. "This is my 'Lake Isle of Innisfree.' You know? 'I hear it in the deep heart's core.'" One hand flitted to her thin chest, held there for a pulse or two. "And the legends, the history . . . why, this is the trysting place of *innumerable* shades." She took a deep breath, apparently planning to rouse some of them.

I stood up. If she was going to start telling ghost stories, I was leaving. I'd already heard them all, pirates, whales, Goodie Hallet and the whole cast of spectral presences hovering in the marshes. Anyway, I had to water my tomatoes and launder a load of towels, so I set my teacup down and went back across the street.

This is a fine place indeed, but you've got to take it as it is—not the way it used to be or should be. Face the bad as well as the good. Enid didn't appear ready to allow for anything short of the ideal. Well, she'd see. The winter nights when not one headlight meets your own for miles, and the coyote's lament sounds as close as that empty space under your deck, yet infinite as the sky. Or the summer Saturdays when you'd rather go without milk for your Wheaties, would even prefer to drape last Christmas's leftover red and green paper napkins over the toilet paper holder than try making a left turn onto Route 6 to buy a pack of Charmin.

She came over a few days later to admire my daffodils. We strolled around to the back of the lot, where she went into raptures about the row of buoys hanging on my shed wall. They're picturesque, all bright and striped; you see them decorating fences and restaurants all the time. Of course, what they're meant to do is mark lobster pots; I can't entirely forget their utilitarian side. I only keep half a dozen that the grandkids dragged back from the beach when they were little. But Jody, Maxie, and Richie are teenagers now; they spend their vacations at soccer or computer camp. Even their parents, my sons and their wives, don't visit every summer as they used to. I have no need for ornamental buoys.

Enid did, though. "I want dozens of them, hundreds. Like that building at Rock Harbor, and that cottage near First Encounter Beach and . . . ."

"Take these, then" I interrupted. "I've always intended to plant hydrangeas there."

She stared, eyes aflutter. "Oh, I couldn't," she said.

"Why not?"

"You're *terribly* kind, but I have to find my own gifts from the sea."

I couldn't see why, and who knows what I'd let myself in for by asking, but luckily, a ringing phone called me into the house just then.

Since she seemed to need so much to belong, I invited her on one of our Wednesday outings. An informal group of us, seniors mostly, residents anywhere from five to seventy years, get together one morning a week to shop or go to a show or museum. Often, we just hit the mall in Hyannis or case the Christmas Tree shop in Orleans, then have lunch in a restaurant. That's how she came to be called Sweet Enid of Eastham. She had this attitude toward everything Cape Cod that made you feel, when she spoke, that your head was full of molasses and honey. She couldn't be critical or even realistic. She persisted in loving what others, more experienced, do not. She even praised traffic rotaries. But like a driver who's never encountered one before, she couldn't seem to enter the circle: the roundel of grousing in which the natives complain about the washashores, the washashores complain about the tourists, the tourists complain about the traffic, and therein they all agree. No, to Enid, Eastham was Utopia. It's annoying to want to vent about an inconvenience and encounter someone whose outlook is all roses and sugar. So the rest of the group started calling her Sweet Enid behind her back.

She was intelligent enough to recognize her misdirection, but even when she tried to be negative, she got it wrong. One June afternoon she told a table full of us how she'd been awakened three nights in a row by a car alarm. "Must be off-Capers," she said.

"Weekly renters," someone agreed. "Think they're still in New York, gotta keep everything under lock and key. Then a raccoon hops on the BMW's hood and all hell breaks loose." Everyone laughed.

Enid could have dropped it there and basked in the glow of being a year-rounder among others of her kind. But she didn't. She treated us all to a reproduction of what she'd heard. "*Tooo-wheet-tooo,*" she trilled, causing adjacent diners to look up sharply. "Just like that, over and over, for a good ten minutes, then it stopped dead. I guess the people who owned the car woke up and turned it off."

Eyes met over clam platters. "This happens every night, just before dawn?" someone asked.

"Yes. You'd think they'd know better than to keep turning their alarm on. Why this is Cape Cod, after all." She gave a short high laugh.

An empty pause. Then the most outspoken among us broke it.

"There's some things can't be blamed on tourists. That's a whippoorwill, dear. What you're hearing is a *bird*. Haven't you ever heard a whippoorwill before?"

Her eyes and mouth widened into three perfect ovals.

I felt sorry for her. "We're not all used to living cheek-by-jowl to an Audubon refuge," I said. "You don't hear whippoorwills where she comes from; you hear traffic and sirens. Right, Enid?"

"A whippoorwill," she murmured, enchantment spreading over her face.

"How sweet," someone said.

Enid nodded enthusiastically.

She tagged along for a few more weeks, then dropped out. She didn't seem upset or reproachful. Maybe the group wasn't what she needed, after all.

I understood that, more or less. I like to be alone on spring nights with my memories, and I like my children to visit one at a time, not fill up the house. There's value in solitude as long as there's not too much of it.

Anyway, Enid still came over to see me pretty frequently. I became the recipient of her confidences. She didn't so much live on the Cape as soak herself in it. She read Beston, Lincoln, Reynard, and Thoreau. She memorized maps, natural histories, tide charts. And by this time, she'd grown quite giddy about those buoys.

She'd found her first one, long sought after, at Coast Guard beach on a green-gray April day. The find carried a slight taint, for someone had already pulled it back near the cliff and dug its pole into the sand so it stood perpendicular like a beacon. She'd wanted hers to be the first hand that scooped it up, still trailing seaweed. Nevertheless, as the buoy was intact, and an arresting neon orange, she hung it on the side of her house facing the road.

That night, she discovered that she could see the curve of Nauset Light's beam, snapping like a kite tail against the clouds. She'd been leaning sideways from her bedroom window to catch a goodnight glimpse of her now properly-bedecked wall.

A huge bounty—three, including a fine red and black stripe—turned up all at once a week later, to her infinite delight. The day after, she informed me that, even with her windows closed, she could hear the sea roaring. Unlikely, since we're a mile from the shore, but I didn't spoil her fun.

Within another month, her wall dripped with buoys. Each time she added another, she got spookier until I began to think she'd gone completely mad.

"Last night," she told me, "I heard sea chanteys. Did you? You must have. There was that breeze, all fish-scented and damp, and the music sailed on it . . . ." She paused to collect herself. "So I went out and bought these." She held up a handful of CD's with whaleboats and seascapes on the boxes. After that, strains full of "Heave away" and "Blow, boys, blow," punctuated with rum and hornpipes, formed the soundtrack of her life. Mine, too, if I spent much time in my front yard. At least it offered some relief from that Patti

Page album she used to play.

I admit I passed this story on to the Wednesday group. "Hard to make it here without connections or a history," we agreed, clucking wisely. "Next thing, she'll claim to have been cavorting with Black Bellamy's ghost . . . ."

She *did* look different. She'd begun to replace the floral prints with Bean denims and flannels that faded more each week. Even her coloring took on the palette of sand, delicate beige and sea-gray. No more liverish blotches or florid pink. The more buoys she hung, the more at ease she seemed. Each, to her mind, had a haunting story to it, of storms and disasters, reunions and bounty. She saw wraiths in the piney mist. She eavesdropped on long-dead Wampanoags and pilgrims.

She got so she'd go on her missions even on moonless nights—I could see her flashlight bobbing down her driveway and onto the path that cuts through the woods to the cliffs and beach. A fisherman friend, up at three to catch the tide, said he saw her a long ways north of the old Coast Guard station, standing on the sand, staring out to sea like a ship's figurehead. Or mad Ahab. I told her this worried me a bit, and she should be careful.

She told *me* that all the lost Cape ships rise from the sea and cruise the shore of the Narrow Land on Midsummer Eve, and that she couldn't wait to see them.

"For heaven's sake," I said. This display of naivete was out of keeping with her years, if not her length of residency. "You're overdoing it."

"Legends come from flesh and bone," she responded.

"What is it you're expecting? Some lost sailor to quaver hallelujah to you from his sea bed?"

She swept me a look of surprise and hurt.

I told her why not just come over early that morning and we'll go out for cranberry pancakes instead?

She said I was a fine Yankee neighbor, but she had already made plans.

Poor Enid, exasperating and pathetic. She reminded me of a buoy with its side staved in, neither useful nor ornamental, destined to lie there making everyone uncomfortable until some good citizen cleans the beach of debris.

Midsummer Day has always seemed a misnomer to me, coming as it does in early summer. But solstices and equinoxes are marked on my kitchen calendar, and I noticed this one because of what Enid had said. The night before brought wind, laden with rain, along with temperatures in the forties. I hoped that meant Enid would behave sensibly. Who'd sit out all night in a Nauset gale? I took myself to a warm bed.

She didn't come round next day, or the next. Her newspapers piled up. I knocked and phoned, got no response, and finally called the police. Enid wasn't there. Enid wasn't anywhere to be found.

Did she drown? Was she abducted? Murdered? God knows it happens, even here. But no body ever turned up. Her doctor testified that she didn't have Alzheimer's. I said she didn't seem depressed. Quite the contrary, she was a walking rhapsody. So was she devoured by coyotes? No one knows. Enid just disappeared.

That was a year ago. There stands her house, empty, starting to smell of mold and mice instead of the potpourri, Seaside Rose, that she bought by the pound. No one knows quite what to do. Mystery seems to be lapsing into myth. Eventually, I suppose, the town or county will take over.

I've been inside that house since her departure. It holds no trace of sadness. Satisfaction is more like it. I thought I heard a gentle chorus of "heave away, heave away." Maybe I'm starting to sound like her, but here's my theory: via spirit fleet or not, she found her Cape Cod welcome. She was absorbed into what she loved so much, became an element herself. Patron saint of the washashores, if you will.

And I'll amend something I said before, that she came to a dreadful end. Now that I've thought about it, it's not dreadful at all. The rest of us, native or not, will probably die in a hospital in Hyannis or Boston, or if we're lucky, at home in our usual four walls. Enid met her end, if that's the right word, with Nauset Light whirling over her and the sea roaring through her dreams. I suggest that she'd been quite right; she did and does belong here as much as the those of the tenth generation, or the dunes, the sandpipers, the fog. Part of the deep heart's core, she might have said.

KELY KNOWLES, "FISHING BOAT"

North Eastham

BY ROBIN L. SMITH JOHNSON

The winter I was seventeen
we lived in a home
with sculpted heads lining the garden.

Such an old place:
the wind shushing in corners,
the trace of other lives.

I made a world of small things.
In the low light after school,
I arranged the minutia of my life:

paper, pen, bookplate, watch.
I'd slip out of my body,
roam the spaces between walls.

Once I couldn't get back in.
My soul doomed to wander—
the air stirred with my shrieking.

A good girl, my teachers said.
What I couldn't see: the light
startling behind the mask.

Moonset, Christmas Eve

BY LESLIE BRETT

The moon sat low on the horizon,
And like a curved feather drifting too close
To a flame, caught fire as it slowly sank into the bay.
It was not even midnight
And we were around the table,
Red wine half gone, half pooled
In glasses marked by our moist fingers and lips
And glimmering, from time to time,
With the reflected lights from the windows.

Just as the moon had started to bend down,
Still white then and strong enough
To light the streets, we entered the old church
On Christmas Eve in Provincetown,
And waited for the familiar story.

This church had heard a thousand stories
Proclaimed from the pulpit and whispered
Behind cupped hands. The children of whalers,
Of artists and travelers, the children of pilgrims,
We paused here in the middle of a hundred tales.
The old dark boards creaked under our feet
And the white walls stood against the wind.
The room filled with the warm air of breathing.

The moon traveled across the sky—
It could have been a star.
And shopkeepers and waiters and lovers
Could have been kings. We waited and sang
And sat close together in coats and scarves.
Every one of us was a shepherd.

By the time the moon was falling low to the edge,
You and I were home again,
An atheist and a Jew, two glasses of wine,
And a radio playing Christmas jazz.
As the reclining crescent set down in the bay
And burned, a celestial ember,
I reached for your hand, thinking
Not even the moon is innocent.

BARBARA MELCHER, "THREE'S A CROWD," WOODCUT

Corn Hill Beach in September

BY LESLIE BRETT

If I could sketch with my pen,
I would draw this:

A wide, wide quiet water
Bordered by a yellow spit of sand and scrub,
A few tall points shooting up to make clear
That man is building here, but never mind.
Soft white clouds rest patiently
In a blue sky, and single gulls curve slowly,
Then swoop from sky to bay.
It is so still, the little breeze
That rustles the hairs around my ears
Is the loudest sound,
And the easy rhythm of the bay
Is like breathing.
I will not even
Turn the pages of my book.

Then, there is the light.
I would draw that, too, if I could,
But I would need more than pen or pencil
To show you the movement,
The clean shimmer
Of the sun on the water,
Like a beaded jacket under stage lights,
And yet, so unlike it,
I can only exhale and try again.

The water is green, then blue,
The water is blue, then green,
The water is white as diamonds,
As it rolls and sighs beside the shore.

Things keep happening, but it doesn't matter.
A plane flies by; a jeep with fishing poles and children
rumbles across the sand.
There are other people here
Who call to one another and laugh,
But it doesn't matter.

If I could sketch this for you
So you could hang it on your wall
In your house on the street in the town
With all the other houses, I would.

A Long and Certain Sight

BY LAUREN WOLK

I am often homesick for a certain shingled house,
attended by tilting pines and the emphatic fragrance of skunks.
Enough land for blueberries and quail, foxes,
even coyote making their unlikely comeback . . .
and for those of us happy to share what is less ours than theirs.

This seems, at first, a silent place,
removed from the slam and clatter of town.
But it approaches the ear differently, waits patiently,
leaps an unguarded synapse,
and then, suddenly . . .

There is the sound of mourning doves,
less song than gentle declaration—"This place is ours."
There is the lush duet of wind and pine, the chime of crickets,
the distant, brassy lament of gulls.
The air here is sharp with pine,
the drift of the sea rising to the sky.
Nothing is lacking here. At every turn, every sense is busy. Content.

I am often homesick for this place.

I am often, elsewhere, struck by the memory of this place.
Something triggers a backward glimpse and I am euphoric,
sick with longing.
The moment passes and I am stranded again, impossibly distant,
as bereft as a yearling sent suddenly on its way.

But now I am back and the sea rises. The stars swing closer.
The unanchored land moves, unimpressed with human borders.
The heaviest weather thrills me. There is nothing that can match it.
A high sea, high wind, high tide put me in my place.
And I am glad to be here.

I am often homesick for a certain shingled house.
It is my mother's.
She knows every growing thing here. Every bird.
The coat of every skunk.
The brutal track of every hurricane that's passed this way.
She likes things wild, unkempt, as they prefer to be.
As they would be if we'd just let them be.
Although she has thwarted, every now and then, the intentions
of tomato worms, stink bugs, and the like . . .
and she's been known, as well, to assist a trumpet vine that's gone astray.
But, on the whole, she's willing to live and let live,
to recognize the wisdom of wild things,
to praise their long and certain sight.

Like me, she prefers a fickle sea. Lazy one day, asurge the next.
She is reassured by this willful sea.
By its fringe of hot, bladed, stinging marsh.
Of bush made rude by thorns, needles, and sucking ticks.
Of fog, all cold and confusion.
Of storms that rage back around, and around, and around before they're spent.
Of dunes that slide down impatiently to meet the sea.
She is reassured by this wildness.

If I am homesick, she is why.
She's kept this place as wild as she could.
It doesn't need taming.

Come In

BY CYNTHIA HUNTINGTON

I have been walking all day in the dunes, and I don't want to come in.
My legs are tired, and my face is burned by the sun.
How can I take any more air into my lungs than is there already?
And how to stop seeing the shimmer of light on the water, the sky so blue?
There are no words here for that blue, and the sand and the birds. . .
How can I leave it all and come inside? All day

I have looked at everything as if I might never see it again.
Knowing that whatever happens, I
will never see everything
or any one thing, exactly like today, in such a shiver of being.
All day I climbed into the spiky branches
of the beach plums, ripping my hands, for the purple,
marble-size fruit hidden there, each as much seed as flesh,

with a taste of cold wind in their darkening juices.
How will I learn to leave these alone? To turn away
as the light keeps on changing and the wind comes up
to throw the waves over, white, then brown. It is already
enough, it must be sufficient, but still I ask for more. . .

The sun will go down in half an hour.
How will I close the door, how will I find my way to bed?
I sit on the hill high above the beach,
watching waves turn, and birds diving below,
every cell in my body drinking this in,
remembering before it can end. I will never

forget any of it. I will always be here. I will not move from this hill.
But then come the deep colours of sunset, rose
and dusky gold, twilight swallowing the world up so gradually, the soft
and softer light. Objects begin disappearing one

at a time, you can't take your gaze away for an instant.
It's gone; my hands are empty . . .
And then the wind, and the beginnings of dark,
then closing the windows to the north, and latching the door,
then only being able to see what is outside, beyond
the windows, not inside where there are shadows.
Then lighting the lamps, the moon coming forward
in the southern sky, the sky moon-washed pale

but the stars over the beach so sharp and clear.
How will I ever be able to close my eyes?
Now Orion rising, one foot out of the ocean,
taking aim at winter; his pose says take cover.
I have been awake all day, and I will sleep,
my body will take me under, and all night in the dark
I will go on breathing this world.

This poem first appeared in Writing Nature, *June 2002*

JOYCE JOHNSON, "DUNE SHACK," PHOTOGRAPH

All Summer Long

BY MARY ELLEN REDMOND

Yesterday my sister made pesto
with basil so pungent
I wanted to kiss it.
Garlic, slippery oil,
in my blender like a processed frog.

Last night the full moon shone
reflecting a large swath across the pond,
like an inviting road. I rose,
walked to the shore
and buried my high school ring,
a photo of my ex and me,
and three wishes. Buried them all
in my grandmother's lace handkerchief,
deep in the sand, their destiny
for the moon and tide to decide.

All summer I become myself again.

Today I plucked blackberries,
pregnant and ripe.
They hung heavy on their bush.
I stuffed them in my mouth greedily,
tongue and lips and fingers stained with blood,
dark purple smear on my clean white shirt.
I don't care.

Dusk, and the ivy on my rafter thrives wildly—
arms reaching out to embrace me.
The light around the pond grows rosy,
air so thick and rich I want to cut it
like a strawberry pie.
My slice of sky.

All summer long I become myself once again.

Seaweed

BY CELIA BROWN

Necklets today, along this shore.
Stuff I once thought of
as mermaid's hair;
a bumper crop overnight;
meshed and airy
as the dream I almost caught.

Now till the turn of the tide
this kelp is ours to own.
As pure clean and transient
the sea winnows here,
separating from sand and shell,
ash and carbon—

"drowning strings,"
I once swam toward in Ireland:
bubble, squeak, pop-your-eyes,
grassy carpets, a slip-and-slide . . .

as strands once green,
now gone to black
become the stuff of our garden;

kelp that curls under water,
that we gather into bins,
vats, laundry pails,
and haul away home over stones.

Walk on the Moon—1969

BY JACQUELINE M. LORING

At noon's low tide along Race Point
on a breathless dirt-bike journey
through hidden paths in shifting sand,
we searched each other for treasures
before the sea returned.

Our giggling lifted us above the mourning
dove, nesting. A red-tailed hawk rose,
circled, plunged toward cresting waves
while we debated, on blowing dunes,
the marsh grass' hold of life.

Our sun-warmed bodies touched
and swam. You lied
about your virginity. I said I understood
enlisting, your father's pride. Gave you
the beach plum blossom from my braid.

You wrapped me in your army blanket,
stoned the waves, placed in my hands
a three-legged star fish,
ordered the incoming
tide to chance and the stars to shine.

"Walk on the Moon—1969" appeared in
Prime Time, December 1999.

Ancient Wisdom

BY ANITA MEWHERTER

I used to know

    how to convert Centigrade to Fahrenheit
    Pythagoras from Euclid
    the Crimean War from the Boer War
    the kings and queens of England, chronologically
    why my participles shouldn't dangle
    and . . .
        how to go from Genesis to Revelation
        without taking a breath

I've forgotten all this . . .
but now I know . . .

    the sweet serenade of peepers flooding the marsh
    the shimmer of sunshine dappling the wall
    fragrance of coffee filling the air
    the tears of a friend held close in my arms
    hum of a yellow cat curled on my lap
    and . . .
        the moth's wing touch of a grandchild's kiss

haiku taxi

poetic musings of a cape cab driver

BY ROSEMARY HILLARD

point A to point B
the story of my journey
take a ride with me

In the late '80s, I was experiencing one of those life crises that assail most of us from time-to-time. Seeking a sense of balance—both mental and physical—I began the study of Tai Chi Ch'uan. I spent countless hours of practice in my backyard in moving meditation. Discipline has never been one of my strong points, but with this I persisted. It helped me focus and center myself—it was my survival tool. Once memorized and internalized, the Tai Chi form (37 sequential postures), like life itself, can be refined through mindful practice. I read the *Tao Te Ching (Book of Integrity and the Way)* by Lao Tzu. I began to make changes in my life, personal and professional, changes that ultimately brought me to settle here in Provincetown.

More recently, I found myself drawn to another Eastern discipline—the writing of *haiku*. Haiku is a Japanese verse form that traditionally consists of seventeen syllables arranged in three lines of 5-7-5 (sets of syllables that can be uttered in one breath) that convey a seasonal feeling and a sense of place or sentiments of emotion. The intent of haiku is to capture the essential quality of an image, an event, or an emotion.

capture the essence
circles cut by windblown grass
weathered grey windfence

I get around. For the past three years I've been driving a taxi in Provincetown, and I love it. I bring to the job 55 years of living, 38 years of driving experience, a B.A. in Studio Art, an M.S. Ed. in Art Therapy, and the skills gained from prior work—as a receptionist, secretary, retail sales clerk, ceramic artist, house painter, sign painter, agricultural laborer, art teacher, public relations specialist, typographer and computer graphics artist, art therapist, HIV educator and counselor. Forever I remain:

an artist, dreamer . . .
a phenomenologist?
i notice small things.

always a student
forever an observer
whatever is meant

Driving a taxi has been the chosen occupation, and source of inspiration, for many a writer (and the focus of a number of movies and television shows). It's a vaguely romantic profession with a kaleidoscopic nature. When business is slow there's time for reflection, reading and writing. When business is brisk there's fast-paced interaction with people and places.

land's end
the things I have seen
Wood End red light, Long Point green
the distance between

I prefer driving the morning shift. Off-season, the streets are quiet as I park the cab, watch the sun rise over the harbor, practice tai chi, and wait for the phone to ring. I wait, watch, listen, feel; changes in light, birds in flight, wind and water. I may have only a few minutes to experience an image/place/feeling/event before I move on. As a form of mental exercise and meditation, I often try to express the essence of that image/place/feeling/event with a haiku.

at dawn
a great blue heron
searching for fish—walks the moors
with regal patience

Inspired by the first annual Provincetown Poetry Festival, held in April, 1999, I put together a tiny chapbook, *Provincetown Haiku* (one sheet of paper folded into a 3" x 3.5" rectangle), containing one haiku for each month of the year. I still carry a few copies with me in the taxi and give them to passengers I intuit will appreciate and enjoy them (copies are also available for sale at Now Voyager bookstore, with half of the $2 cost going to Helping Our Women and the Soup Kitchen in Provincetown).

dunes
listen, understand
always the sound of the wind
reshaping the sand

I don't always follow the rules (of course not!) and I don't always rhyme, though the challenge of rhyme is often irresistible to me.

searching
sticks, stone, shells and bone
fragments found on a pathway
i travel alone

In my work as a cab driver I interact with all types of people. I've had passengers from 5 to 95 years of age, preschool to Ph.D., people of all professions and no profession, natives as well as visitors from all corners of the world. I know my "regulars" by name, recognize their voices on the telephone, know which door they come out of, how they like things done, and where they're likely to be going at any given time (work, school, shopping, etc.) There's something very comforting about this small town familiarity and I enjoy the more leisurely pace of winter when I can spend some extra time visiting and helping people with their errands. All the cabs in Provincetown operate on a fixed rate of $3 per person anywhere within the town limits, $4 per person to Herring Cove, and $5 per person to the airport or Race Point. The rates haven't changed in years, and are affordable enough to offer door-to-door mobility for residents and visitors alike. Most people give me a tip in addition to their fare. Tips are ordinarily cash, but I've had some unconventional tips too—a banana, a muffin, a freshly baked scone, an ear of corn, fresh fish (right off the boat), scratch tickets, kind words, and words of wisdom

. . . as part of a tip
he gave me some tomatoes
warm and ripe and red

—priceless gifts of gratitude—

tips on how to live
a long, full and joyful life
celebrate each day

One of the designated taxi stands in town is in front of the Chamber of Commerce down by the wharf and I always enjoyed watching the pigeons that would roost on the roof. Whenever a car turned the corner or a loud noise startled them, the birds would lift as one, circle the parking lot, and return to their perch. After a short spring vacation, I returned to find only a few birds left—survivors of an extermination campaign by the Chamber—and in response I wrote the following linked haiku:

rock doves
(rules to break)

if you feed the birds
they begin to congregate
they roost on the roof

the wind ruffles their feathers

infinite variety
plump iridescent pigeons
cooing in the sun

i turn and cover my eyes,

startled by the sound
of a thousand beating wings
rising to the sky

In haiku, constrained to so few syllables, choice of words is critical. Ever since I began
to read I've had a fascination with dictionaries. Even when I feel I have a good grasp of
meaning, I like to look up a word to see what other definitions may be attached to it.
Sometimes I discover that the word I've chosen is totally inappropriate for my purpose
(I'm more dreamer than scholar). Other times I discover that the word is not only
perfect, but provides imagery and meaning on more than one level. "Rock Doves," as
originally published in *Provincetown Magazine,* was followed by a list of related
definitions, intended to make a social comment over and above the experiential nature
of the haiku itself. For example: the shifting color (iridescence) of the pigeons is
apparent only when seen from different angles (different points of view). The soft
murmuring sound that pigeons make (coo) is synonymous with speaking gently and
lovingly. To rest, sit or sleep on a perch/roof (roost) can be expanded to include "rule
the roost" or "come home to roost," implying repercussions, especially disagreeable
ones that may boomerang (just as the pigeon extermination did for those who ordered
it).

Anyone who has tried to navigate Commercial Street at the height of the tourist
season knows how congested it gets. Driving can be a real challenge—dodging pedestrians, bicyclists and other obstacles. My dispatcher (coincidentally named Pigeon)
choreographs my journey; the rhythm of a summer day is fast, flexible and efficient.
"What's your progress? . . . Where are you now?" All day long I keep the radio tuned to

classical music—it has a calming effect (on me, at any rate) and I've yet to have anyone complain. On a busy summer day, driving the cab can be stressful, exhausting and intense:

Blessing of the Fleet
kamikaze bicycles
two-way one-way street

but blessedly concrete:

tell me where you are
and where you would like to be
let me take you there

I hope you've enjoyed the ride.

JOYCE JOHNSON, "SALT POND, EASTHAM," WOODCUT

Prelude at Eastham

BY MARILYN BENTOV

At first the late light brushes
honey ochre rust
across the dunes and down
to seas a long way out.

On this deep shore horses fly
flinging waters
torn from ebb tide
ribboning through miles of sand

particles that mirror sunset fire.
Houses turn gold.
Dusk hesitates—
Night hides in wisps of cloud.

People from the houses sitting
on the dunes stand
in silence. Watch.
A boy walks out to where

the water sews a seam of light
between the sea
and land. He draws a bow
across a violin.

July

MARY DOERING

all summer
my eyes face east
full of ocean
wild and blue
but I know the blackness
under waves
that knock me down
know the part
that takes breath away
the numbing cold
even in July

still, that blue loops round my wrist
face open as a child's
saying come with me
and even though I know
I go

once, I tried to dive under the waves
time it just right
but fear made me cautious
and I never got the rhythm
either diving too soon
or waiting too long
my body heavy, salty
stiff as an old dog

in the marsh
a blue heron
balances on one leg

she has learned to walk
across mud flats without sinking
moving lightly
over the charcoal and bone
of three million years
her long neck extended
watching for signs of life

KAREN NORTH WELLS, WATERCOLOR

The Tourist

BY ROSE GOTSIS

She drives over the bridge
leaving behind
the woman
whose heartbeat is connected
to a measured reality
of tangible or intangible needs
of those she loves.

Beyond the crook
of Cape Cod's neck,
she lives with unmade beds,
unmatched cups and saucers,
and talks to the gulls
she can see through openings
of her weathered wooden walls.
Mornings, she walks the beach
to search for plover nests
and washed-up shells.

Later, you'll find her sitting
on the sand,
reading seamy paperbacks, or staring
Zen-like at the ocean's horizon,
until she is wrapped in a seaweed of dreams.

By the time the hot-pink sun
drops into Rock Harbor,
she has discarded the deadlines
that choked her,
and rediscovered the lifeline
that keeps her mindful of why she is here
one more year.

Hurricane at Cape Cod

BY LOIS EDWINA GRAYSON

The signs were there,
The leaves rustled,
How still the birds,
Humid and grey the day.
The quiet was ominous,
The shades drawn,
The glass could give way

Fifteen-foot swells
They warned,
It could come at high tide,
It might sweep the dunes—
Little children, little children
Stay home with mommy and daddy
In the basement
By the furnace,
Still, there seemed no safe place to hide

The storm was relentless
Powerful,
It pounded the sea,
The rollers came
Gun metal
Foreboding
Alien
One after another,
Like an advancing army

We would not get the brunt of it—
The tide was low
When the ponderous gusts came,
Yet, the trees toppled,

Roofs were sheared,
Boats foundered

The aftermath was grueling
The handsome Cape
Was severely maimed

There is reconciliation, peace howe'er,
When man yields
To the strength of the blow,
He bends as one
With one another
Like the scrubby Cape Cod pine,
And thus survives,
Head bowed,
It is beyond his slender control.

"The gentle Cape Cod pine survived, but the tall, brittle locust tree did not. The locusts fell en masse."

ILLUSTRATION BY LOIS EDWINA GRAYSON.

I I

The Making of Generations

Water Music

BY MARCIA PECK

Chapter Seven: Lessons

SUMMERS, GROWING UP ON CAPE COD, I learned to play the cello. Daddy said that if I practiced the cello an hour a day in winter, I could do two in summer. With a good teacher I could accomplish twice as much in half the time. He said that summer was precisely when you *had* the time to work hard, and that by doing so, maybe someday I'd get good enough to learn the crown jewel of all the cello repertoire, the Dvorak Cello Concerto.

For the strides I would be making the summer of 1956, an outstanding teacher was needed, even if my father didn't know where the money was going to come from. I was eleven, and could begin to study in earnest. And so to help me on my path toward the Dvorak Cello Concerto, he placed my musical education in the hands of Alphius Metcalf, an elderly man who came from Boston each summer and took a room at Rose Acres Cottage in Wellfleet. My mother would drive me. She liked Wellfleet, with its widows' walks and antique stores.

On the day of my first lesson she turned off Route 6 and steered up the tree-lined blacktop. The buildings were low slung, modestly hugging the rise as if to avoid attracting the attention of ocean winds that sculpted the dunes in nearby Truro.

She parked in front of the First Congregational, which had the only steeple clock in the world that struck ship's bells. We were early, and so I slipped my hand into hers and we walked up Main Street. The shops were white clapboard. Unlike the standard Cape Cod weathered shingle, clapboard had to be painted, which made Wellfleet seem impractical but cared for. She stopped in front of Windward Antiques, the one building whose paint was blistered and beginning to peel.

We went inside.

Windward Antiques was chockerblock full. There were framed botanical prints, tarnished brass instruments of navigation, furniture smelling of beeswax, breakable lamps with frayed silk shades, pewter items of all kinds, a tattered lace shawl, and a mottled clock face without its case. A bell tinkled and dust motes flurried as I closed the door behind me. My mother stepped tentatively across the plank floor toward a porcelain figurine standing on a drop leaf table.

Something stirred behind a desk in one corner of the room, a wrinkled woman wearing sensible shoes and a fresh dusting of face powder. A small noise, half rattle, half purr, emanated from her by way of greeting.

My mother's hand, which she had reached out to touch the figurine, hovered uncertainly, and strayed instead toward her hair. She didn't pause over the luster of old wood or run her hand across a cool porcelain surface when people were watching. It was too personal. She nodded and idly picked up an iron trivet.

"Looking for anything special?" asked the antique behind the desk.

"No. Thank you. In fact we can't stay." She set down the trivet and turned toward the door.

And at that moment I discovered, on a shelf beneath a large gilt mirror, a fan. A fan made of ostrich feathers, closed and stuck in a dusty glass vase. Six plumes, that spilled extravagantly over the rim. I thought it was the most lavish thing I had ever beheld. It was a musty pink color, and in it I saw not merely a dress-up accessory, but—as they would say in the courts of Europe—a true accoutrement. A sort of royal scepter and magic wand, all in one.

"Oh," I breathed. I reached for it gingerly.

"Dust-catcher," said my mother from the doorway.

"Six dollars," said the wrinkled woman. "It's very old."

I turned pleading eyes toward my mother.

"Six dollars for that? That's a dollar a feather."

"Please?" I begged.

"Are you coming?"

I hesitated.

She turned and left, letting the door swing shut behind her. The bell tinkled loudly in the silence that followed. I watched her tuck her purse under her arm, look up and down the street as if trying to remember what came next, and then turn and walk past the window, without a glance inside.

I stood for a moment. I stole a look at the woman in the corner, convinced that if I made the bell ring again, she would be annoyed. But I couldn't help it.

"Good bye," I mumbled, opened the door and shut it quickly behind me.

And that was that. To tell the truth, I think that even more than I wanted the fan, I wanted my mother to want me to have it.

·

We took my cello from the car in silence and walked the half block off Main Street. Rose Acres was an ancient looking cottage so shaded by an enormous maple tree that passing through the vine-covered picket fence was like entering a cave. My mother made me shake the sand out of my shoes and tap them against the stone stoop before I entered. Inside, murmurs of conversation, like lullabies, reached us as we passed the parlor and creaked up the thinly carpeted stairs to Mr. Metcalf's room on the second floor. We didn't speak until we had gained his doorway. Mr. Metcalf was a guest, and we were guests of *his*. We came and left as if our right to be there was a tenuous one.

She knocked. The door opened and Mr. Metcalf stood smiling at me. Indeed, a smile was practically his only expression.

From the cool, dark interior of the central hallway we emerged into his gabled corner room. I had met few people as old as Alphius Metcalf. He had not missed a summer at Rose Acres since the Depression. He was tall and willow slender. His eyes were round—he had the perpetually startled look of a seagull—and each pale iris was fogged by a creamy film.

Nearly everything about him was white: his skin the color of typing paper; his linen vest and trousers; the porcelain wash basin and water jug; the painted spool bed and chenille bedspread, unwrinkled and geometrically straight. He had a long, tapered nose, the bones of which were covered so transparently that it looked as if he had barely enough skin to reach to its tip. On the far side of the room an eyelet curtain had been looped to one side of the open window which faced the big maple outside. That tree must have been a music lover, because its branches pressed right up to the casement. The room smelled of lavender water.

"Ah, Mrs. Grainger, so nice to meet you." Mr. Metcalf bobbed and bowed to my mother. They exchanged "how-do-you-do's" and "um's" and "yes indeed's," and I could see that, whatever she had expected, he was an improvement on it. She asked him to call her Lydia, and then she took up her position on a small wooden chair beside the bedstead. She began to knit.

"And you must be Lily. My dear." Mr. Metcalf clasped his hands together as he surveyed me. "We have lots to do. *Lots* to do." He said this as if it pleased him no end, and was sure I would feel exactly the same.

I was doubtful. But there was something infectious about his optimism. And he seemed truly unaware that he was unmistakably odd.

I unpacked my cello. "We have wonderful things to work on this summer," he continued, and patted a stack of étude books on his dresser with evident glee.   "There is Dotzauer and Popper. Oh, and Sevcik. We mustn't overlook our technique. Without technique, we can make no music . . ."

Mr. Metcalf's voice rustled on, like tulle in ballet costumes.

I liked him. He had a gentle, weightless way. It seemed a simple thing, to try to play the right fingers in the right order and have him say, "Why Lily, that's fine. So fine. I can see you are going to do excellent work. Oh, this is going to be such a summer!"

He kept in constant motion, demonstrating, admonishing, encouraging, cajoling. His dry fingers curled over my right hand, correcting Mr. Furia's stiff old-fashioned position, steering and molding my fingers into a living, breathing bow grip. "Tension banished. *Now* the music can sing. Once again." He conducted my phrases, stabbing the air with his bony knuckles, eyes lifted heavenward, and his long nose sailed past my shoulder like the prow of a ship.

At the end of my lesson he said that each week, if I played well, he would do a trick for me. He asked if I had ever heard the magnificent call of the Ruby Throated Warbler.

I hadn't.

Then that *must* be today's trick. He trilled and whistled and jiggled his Adam's Apple with his forefinger until it sounded like a whole lexicon of birds.

On the way home my mother said sternly that music should be its own reward and, anyway, she had never heard of a Ruby Throated Warbler.

But I could tell she really liked Mr. Metcalf. It was to let me know she was no pushover.

•

My parents fought about two things that summer: money and in-laws. And the sound of their fights began to form a regular accompaniment to my morning practicing.

By mid-July my fingers were more callused than my bare feet. I was making progress—Mr. Metcalf said so—but it wasn't going fast enough. Every day Daddy took time out from typing to check on me. He came in one morning just as I had gotten all twisted up.

"What's this, Lily? Getting a little ahead of yourself?" He—and the faint scent of fresh pine sap—sat down on the cot next to me. "Slow down. Slow down. Try it ten times. But slowly."

I made little tic tac toes in the sand on the floor with the tip of my bow. He was full of pointers, but they all boiled down to one thing: repetition. He wasn't so interested in the subtle little habits that made practice time productive. He had more faith in total time served. An uncomplicated method and, in his estimation, universally effective.

I blew sand from the tip of my bow, placed it on the strings and began. I was on the third repetition when we heard my mother dragging the metal laundry tub, scraping it up the path to the clothesline. Daddy left.

I added a pencil mark to the row of slashes in the margin of my music.

"Need help?" I heard him ask.

I started my fourth repeat. By the fifth their voices had risen. I could hear them clearly over my sixteenth notes.

Where were we going to get the money to finish our cottage? my mother wanted to know. Daddy wanted to ask her parents. We had workmen to pay.

"We could cut back," she said.

"You should have said that last spring," he said.

I took the pencil and marked a slash for number five and started again.

"They can afford it. Your father would want to help if he knew we were in trouble."

"*Are* we in trouble?" said my mother.

"No."

"Why don't you ask your own parents if it's such a good idea?"

He said that was a laugh. He said it didn't take brains to know that his parents didn't have any money.

He had done it now. Sure enough, she began to strafe him with words like "threadbare" and "pinch penny." I played louder to drown her out. But over the music I still heard "can't manage our affairs" and "humiliate me" and "just so you can call them tight-fisted."

Then my father's voice burst in. "That's right," he said. "Tight-fisted. You bet she is. I can't make it up to you that Bertha Melrose cares for no one but herself."   He was yelling now. He said it was a mystery to him how such a selfish person as Bertha Melrose gave birth to so fine a woman as my mother. It was her one act of generosity, he said.

I put my cello down and went to the door of the tent. "Stop shouting!" I could feel the ridges left by the steel string on my fingertips.

My mother shifted her head ever so slightly to include me in her vision. Eyebrows arched. She let a Bob White whistle fill in the silence. Then she said, eyes narrowed, "I see I have a daughter who likes to interfere."

"It's all right, Lily." My father found his voice. "Finish your practicing."

I looked from one to the other.

"It's all right, cowgirl," he said again. "I'll be there in a minute."

I went back inside and picked up my cello, the cello on which one day maybe I'd play the Dvorak Cello Concerto. I thought it was generous of my father to blame their fights on Bertha Melrose when my mother's attacks were so mean.

"Lydia . . ." My father's pleading voice moved slowly down the path. I stopped playing. A door slammed. It slammed again. Then there was silence. I had lost track of which number I was on. I started over. Nothing worked right. My bow scraped the wrong string and my fingers stumbled against each other. When I looked up, Daddy was in the doorway, pinched and threadbare. Pretending everything was all right.

"I'll get it, Daddy," I said. He didn't answer. I played the measures again.

"No." He rubbed his lame leg. "No, Lily. Do it again."

I tried again.

"Better." But it wasn't better. "You should do that section until I say stop."

I played the passage two or three times through; then he left. Sometimes when he came to the tent, he would smile. "Got the wind at your back today, eh Lily?" he would say, and his smile made me forget that we didn't have enough money.

I repeated the bars over and over. He didn't come back. I tried playing each note ten times in a row, then the next note, making the passage ridiculously simple. Hoping he would catch me at that game. I listened for him. Nothing. I tried it backwards. I traced the shadow of a pine bough on the tent wall with the tip of my bow. He had vanished. Finally I packed up. I looked in the playhouse, the new house, the outhouse. At last I checked the knoll, where he did his writing. No typewriter tapping.

When I crested the hill I spotted him under the black oak, legs splayed on a blanket, playing solitaire.

•

To get to Wellfleet, we had to pass Blackfish Creek, named for the pilot whales which periodically stranded in the shallows along the shore north of Eastham. It was said that they beached themselves deliberately and died, not from lack of food or water, but from their own body weight, pressing on their lungs and heart. I had heard that the mates of stranded whales were known to linger in the waters offshore long after there was no hope their partner would ever swim again. People who lived in the area knew this because they heard the singing, lonely songs of animals who lived in the ocean but were mammals like us.

No one drove that stretch of road without looking for the whales, no matter how long it had been since the last stranding.

In late July the *Cape Codder* reported that a pod of mothers and juveniles had been discovered milling in the shallows, the first in a number of years. Townspeople—with a certain amount of pride that theirs was the chosen beach—had convened their small flotilla of skiffs and trawlers and herded or towed as many as they could out to sea. There was a photo on the front page. The rest were trapped when the tide went out and abandoned on the beach to die.

These were the ones my mother and I saw on the way to my lesson that afternoon. The day I found out we were in trouble because Daddy said No, we weren't. The hopeless cases. It was hot and Route 6 was empty. As we approached the old Wharf Road, my mother slowed down. We could see eight black mounds looming out of the shallows, like the hulls of grounded ships. She stopped the car on the shoulder and let it idle for a minute. No one was around. It was hard to see anything clearly. She squinted in the direction of the whales, then looked up and down the road. She chewed her lip. Finally she turned off the ignition.

"I suppose I should take a look," she said, as if to do her duty.

I popped open my door.

"You stay here," she said.

"Please?" I begged.

"I'll be right back."

She crossed the road and stood at the edge of the water, hand indecisively on her hip.

"Can you see anything?" I called.

She glanced at me momentarily and then reached down to remove her shoes. I got out of the car and crossed the road. She was out on the flats by the time I got my shoes off and waded out to her.

"I thought I told you to stay in the car." She scowled. Then her whole face shrank at the smell. "Stay close, you understand?"

I nodded.

We hiked up our shorts and waded out to the first whale, smaller than I expected, and tipped partly on its side. Fiddler crabs scuttled from under my feet. A couple of horseshoe crabs moved at a prehistoric pace through the shallow water, dragging one brutal spike—a tail? a rudder? We were near the naval base at Quonset Point, and a plane buzzed in the distance, flying low. The tide was going out. There were white splotches all over the whale. A puss wound on its back expelled a swarm of flies, which fanned out like fireworks, and settled back down again. Two expressionless eyes, partially submerged, were filming over. My mother moved around it, keeping a distance and averting her face. She went on to the next one.

I followed her to each dead whale, unsure if there were rules to follow, a protocol for visiting whales with no more chances. The Catholics would know what to do, but there were none to ask.

"This one's alive," said my mother. She was standing by the whale furthest from shore. She moved in closer to it and poked its dry black skin tentatively with her finger. She bent down and looked into its face and then scooped some water up in her shirttail and flung it over the whale. Its head became a glistening black watermelon. The whale moved a slender, pointed fluke. It was alive. She nudged it with her foot. "Swim, baby. Go on, swim."

I thought a sound came from the animal. "Mom, I don't think . . ."

She nudged it harder. "Lily, help me."

She leaned a shoulder into the dark mass. "Swim," she urged. I splashed it with water, and pushed with her. It was stuck fast. We could sooner have pushed Cape Cod to Block Island, the two of us. "Go on. Swim!" my mother got sterner. In the distance I could hear the guns at the naval base, low and dissonant, like someone laying his forearms on the bottom notes of a piano. She looked up in that direction and shaded her eyes. "Damn it, swim!" She slid her hand into the whale's mouth and tugged on its jawbone.

"Let's go, Mom. We can't do anything."

A car on the road slowed.

"You can swim," she demanded. She strained against the thick skin. She stepped back. To take stock. To start over.

"It's no use, Mom," I cried. "Let's go."

"Need some help?" a man called from the road.

She dug her shoulder into the whale's side.

"It's okay," I called uncertainly. Daddy would know what to do. Dodie would know what to do. Even Aunt Fanny would know what to do.

"Let's go now. We should go. Mama?"

The car drove away.

Her hands clenched. Her jaw worked. "Swim!" she ordered again.

At that moment I saw us as if from far overhead, up to our knees in water on the edge of a sand dune, Cape Cod, the easterly most point of the United States. Fragile as a piecrust. Far out to sea.

"You're being . . ." I floundered. "Daddy would not like this."

And then she kicked it. Her foot went out. Water sprayed us.

I tried to step between her and the whale. "Get out of here!" she shouted. At me or at the whale, I wasn't sure which. She dug both feet into the sand and shoved against it.

"Mother." My voice trembled.

But my mother seemed not to know I was there. Another car passed. The whale didn't care about either of us.

"Mother!" I said again. Louder.

"It's none of your business," she said to the daughter who liked to interfere. She drew her leg back—preparing to punish whales who wouldn't save themselves—and momentarily wavered on the other foot, seeking her balance in the water. Her shorts were wet up to the waist.

"Stop it!" I cried.

I caught hold of her foot. We fell into the water. She twisted and thrashed. Salt stung my eyes. I threw myself on top of her and tried to pin her arms.

"Leave me alone," she shrieked. Fury had grabbed her like an undertow, deeper and deeper. Her foot jerked to her chest, a wedge against me.

"Daddy's girl," she spit at me. She shoved me from her. Her knee caught me in the stomach, but it was her words, her saved-up hope-splitting words, that made me gasp for breath.

"Stop," I tried to say, but it came out choked.

She went slack. I tried to get up but stumbled on top of her. She pushed me away. I rolled off her, coughed, and leaned back against the whale, whose heart still beat, however faintly, but I didn't care anymore. I elbowed, hard, the thick carcass, scornful it had stopped trying.

"Stupid fish," my mother hissed.

"It's not a fish," I said, spitefully.

She picked up a handful of wet sand. I flinched, but she heaved it past me and it hit the whale with a tired slap. Without any force or will in the arm that threw it.

The whale made a soft downward noise, almost a sigh. And from the bay, some ways out, I heard a cry of utter loneliness, a solo voice, like a cantor wailing, but less earthly, rising and falling, a plainsong which seemed too pure a grief to come from anything merely mortal. It seemed connected only to sadness itself.

"I know it's not a fish," she said.

Back at the car I held still while my mother scoured my head dry with a towel. Her lips moved, forming words, but she said nothing out loud. She made me take off my wet clothes and put on my bathing suit. She did the same. She took the towel to my body, hard like sandpaper. The towel hurt. Her hands hurt me. It made me glad. It put our hurts together, skin to skin.

I took my lesson in my bathing suit. Mr. Metcalf never said a word. Afterwards my mother took me into Windward Antiques and bought me the ostrich plume fan.

"Don't tell your father," she warned. I think she meant about the six dollars.

DRAWING BY KELY KNOWLES

Twenty-One

BY GAYLE HEASLIP

I smelled you in my sleep
Twelve hours old
Kronkite was on the hospital TV
You lay on my chest
Your head fragile with new bone and tissue
Your eyes strong and calm

I was so pleased to meet you

If you were four today
I'd give you a hand-sewn doll
Gingham dress, lace petticoat
And a soft knit blanket to wrap her in

You'd be pleased to take her to bed
Where you'd lay
Comforted in mother love
Wrapped in prayer

If you were twelve today
I'd give you fine writing paper
Colored inks and artists' pens
Stamps to border every page
And a box to seal it to yourself

You'd be pleased to know I saw you
from the side
My prayers accompanying you
from the side

You are twenty-one today
My hands are empty of gifts to please you

Still, in the mail I sent a leaf
The fiery colors of October on its glassy surface
It drifted down the states to your Georgia address

Does it please you?

You stand in a waterfall of prayer
Proud and beautiful
Dry as a bone

On my knees
My blessing to you today
As fragile in your hands as glass
As strong as fire

Adding some words to my mother's gravestone

BY JUNE BEISCH

"Well, I don't know," said the gravestone
carver at Mt. Hope Cemetery in Ashland, Wisconsin.
"That'll cost you. Words don't
come cheap, you know. And the original
sentiment is usually the best."

When the aged voice went off to find a pen,
I thought about the sad
transactions of headstones, the
business of perpetual care.

Say that I loved life, my mother once
said to me. *Write it on my gravestone.*
How could I have forgotten this?

Say that she loved life and say
that all of her children danced in her light.
Say anything, but do not write
Here Lies the Body of.

Was this a failure of the imagination
or are these just the most expedient words?
*Say that men must endure their going hence
even as their coming hither.* Say that

*life is a bridge, go over it — but do not
install yourself on it.* Say what the poets
and prophet say, but in a new way.

Always I remember her out in front
tying up morning glories with a string
outside our old apartment

in South Minneapolis wearing
her sleeveless cotton dress in summer
and short hair which was the fashion,

struggling along as a single mother
longing for a life more eloquent. Say
that she loved life, that simple sentiment,

and say that all of her children danced in her light.

HEATHER BLUME, INK DRAWING

Body Language

ELIZABETH SWANSON GOLDBERG

for Marcelle

As if drawn I move
to stroke my newly heavy belly
rhythms unscripted,
inspired like the moment of perfect connection
      that is a poem in the making;
uttered like words even as I speak
other conversations with partners more present,
partners who respond in kind.
Our talk, different, is more penetrating:
your messages rapid, clean, singular,
bubbling upward like balloons let fly
into the inner air of my flesh.
Odd shaped balloons,
bouncing as they do on ceilings at celebrations
with no further to go, sliding across the surface,
clinging with the force of electricity.
Trapped, it would seem.
Yet what is the freedom of open air to a balloon
      but certain death?

And this is what I fear for you.
As we speak through our different tongues
I feel already the loneliness of loss,
the pull of grief like the back side of a coin,
weighted, always present,
a sure bet with random timing.
We will leave each other as absolutely
as we share air, blood, and water
today, daughter within daughter,
curving Chinese boxes.

So I rub my joy at holding you safe
            out over my belly,
a circular pattern that you answer
with kicks like carnival,
and I feel in this time that I have triumphed,
bottled joy inside my body like a jar—
if only until the lid bursts,
the coin lands,
the balloon floats out into the waiting sky.

KAREN KLEIN, INK DRAWING

Rooted

BY WENDY LEVINE

FOR THE PAST TWO WEEKS I have done nothing but empty and clean out the gray, shingled saltbox where I spent summers as a girl.

Just after five in the morning I walk barefoot up the back of our sand dune to catch the sun-up and say good-bye. I carry warm coffee in a white, throw-away, Styrofoam cup.

Over the last fifteen years, like a pup needing affection, part of the dune crept closer, and now lies snugged in, almost touching the beach plum and bayberry in the yard behind the kitchen.

I reach the top of our dune. Lavender inches over the horizon, brushing the sky, preparing it for the coming of the day.

Then, as I have always done, I claim as mine everything I see, the bay waters from Truro to Boston, the coast line curving in front of the Beach Point cottages and swinging around to meet the ocean at the old lighthouse at the tip of the Cape, the Pilgrim Monument, the Pamet harbor, and every fishing boat in sight.

"My girls will miss all this," I say.

I remember my cousin Emily's stuttering delight when, long ago, we reached this spot and she saw the ocean for the first time.

I was about eight when Mother convinced her sister Ada to let us borrow her daughter Emily for the summer. That way, being an only child, I would have someone to play with on rainy days and at the beach while Mother lay on the sand, eyes closed, listening to Daddy read Dickens.

Until Emily fell in love with some boy, she came to the Cape every summer. It became our ritual to race up and down the highest dune on Ballston Beach, gasping with laughter, shoving ahead of each other, elbows jammed into bellies, braids unraveling, hunks of cheese and salami crushed in the heat of our hands and dropping through our fingers, to lie as sand-coated litter.

Sharp dune grasses flick and sting my legs in their senseless attempt to uproot themselves and follow the wind across the empty beach. The ninnies, they ought to know by now that they were born to be nested in, put here to grip the sand and hold it down . . . not to runaway, to give up their place and disappear.

I burrow my toes close to their roots and spill the last drops of coffee over their heads.

Crushing the cup into the pocket of my slacks, I walk back to the house for a final check before the long drive back to Manhattan.

Just before I graduated from Barnard over 20 years ago, Daddy died. When I married Tim, Mother left the city and moved to Truro so she could live near the beach, quietly and alone.

After her long illness the house was legally mine. Even though I knew I would have to sell—Tim and I agreed to keep the stocks invested for the girls' college tuition and use the money from the house to pay estate taxes—I am not ready to hand the house over to strangers.

Howland Jr., however, the most tenacious son-of-a-bitch realtor around, is eager to expel me. He has been calling for days, his voice contentious, sharp. He wants me out this morning.

"The new owners want to take possession, don't ya know. They want to take it all apart, do everything over for their daughter's wedding on the Fourth of July, don't ya know!"

I sit down at the kitchen table and wipe my toes with a paper towel, still mindful not to spill sand all over the floor.

The house is finally "broom clean" as stipulated. But the kitchen needs painting. I squelch a ridiculous impulse to leave a note suggesting they keep the color as is, lemon yellow. I walk through the dining room into the entrance hall where bright blue and green ceramic pots filled with daisies from the garden used to stand on either side of the door.

Instead of flowers, I count seven stiff, brown cartons.

Mother kept it all. Photographs jumbled with old medical reports in cardboard boxes. Tax returns and letters from camp tied together with white string. Envelopes filled with burnished gold, bejeweled, '50s screw-on earrings. The carved mouse I made in fifth grade stuck under a pile of pink and beige bras. "Mix and mismatch" had been her credo.

I devoted three days to organizing her drawers. Packing up. Throwing out. I kept her garden gloves and a few rags she used for drying paintbrushes, still stained with the vivid colors of her palette. In her dark closet, crammed with winter and summer clothes sharing hangers, tangled together, I pushed my face into her knit sweaters and inhaled the musty odor of fog and sea stones and the residual vapors of turpentine.

I filled boxes and labeled each one with a red magic marker: Shoes, Coats, Summer, Winter, and then stacked them in the hall ready for the swap shop and other people's closets.

Suddenly I want out! Running to check the den, my foot twists in a crack between the floorboards. I fall. Going down I see myself reflected in the mirror above the antique school desk where we always dropped the mailbox key, and I remember falling in front of that mirror once before.

I was five, standing on the piano stool, stretching up tall to see myself braiding my hair for the first time. My earliest memory of accomplishment.

I will take the mirror, not leave it behind as I had planned.

Limping into the living room, I sink into the couch and lean back, taking deep breaths, waiting for my foot to stop throbbing.

Last night out of pride, wanting "them" to find the house bright and beautiful, I raised the white linen shade which my mother always insisted kept the fabrics from fading, and exposed the room's most important feature, the picture window.

Through it I now see the night lights of Provincetown dissolve in early morning clouds.

When I was about six, my father had the window installed as a special gift for Mother who was a dedicated artist but always complained that she'd never be famous because the room was too damn dark.

I was sitting right here on the couch the day the window was hung and Mother saw it for the first time. She came back from a swim, her legs damp and sandy, a yellow and white striped towel around her neck. She let out a wild whoop and grabbed Daddy's face in her hands, kissing his lips over and over again until he had to hold her off to catch his breath.

"Oh my God, my dearest darling! It's so wonderful! You're so wonderful!"

The brilliance of the light and the turquoise waters of the bay pulled the room to the brink of the beach. She swung Daddy into a dance, careening around the furniture, almost knocking two watercolor landscapes right off the walls.

That night we cheered my mother's certain celebrity with large chocolate ice cream cones from the wharf in Wellfleet.

Every morning during the summer vacation my father played golf while my mother stood at her easel in the living room, painting until lunch time.

Before the window was installed, there had been just a wall. I couldn't see Mommy at all so I played by myself, waiting for Daddy to come home and for her to quit doodling around and take me swimming.

Most mornings I spent the time walking around the house digging under things, looking for buried coins, wishing I had a best friend. On hot days I turned on the hose, spraying water all over myself and the cat.

Then the window arrived and the whole wall opened up. Suddenly I could see Mommy painting, humming softly to piano music from a small, black radio on the book shelf. I watched her move back and forth in front of her easel, her eyes examining the canvas. I giggled as she pushed her head from one side to the other, frowning, rubbing her nose, shading her eyes with the back of her hand. Then she smiled, captured by her visions.

Even though I wasn't supposed to I ran and stood beside her watching her press color onto the canvas with a stubby palette knife.

"Mommy, can I paint with you?" I asked.

"Go play," she said. "This is my time."

So I went outside, sitting alone on the porch step, on the other side of the window, looking in. I waved my hand but she didn't see me. I was afraid she would never see me again.

The window threw my frightened expression back at me. Glistening in the sunshine, it dared me to peer through its hard glass to see what I was missing. It captured my voice so Mother couldn't hear me call. It couldn't be raised, even a few inches, to let me crawl inside.

Every day I ran my hand across its tight, smooth face, squinting and searching for some tiny fissure that I could pick and chip and make big enough to wiggle my finger through and remind Mommy that I was there.

Although it looked fragile, like ordinary glass, allowing Mother to look across the bay to Plymouth, the window was a demon, keeping my mother for itself while I sat mute, still as a stick, a small shingle, nailed in place.

Not even having the nerve to pick up a stone.

Here I sit again, quietly confronting my old enemy. A gull shrieks, as if the window has stolen a voice to mock me. Infuriated, I ignore the pain in my foot, run to the kitchen, open the cabinet underneath the sink and reach for the heavy iron hammer.

DRAWING BY SABINA TEICHMAN

Gathering Fruit

BY ELIZABETH SWANSON GOLDBERG

for RWS

Flowering plants create seed pods
in order to propagate themselves in nature.
Clipping the seed pod of a flowering plant in a garden setting
conserves energy for next year's blooms.
—RWS

I didn't know what a garden meant
until I made one.
And then, through the long lens of retrospect—
a vision denied as it happens,
available only as a kind of pastness—
the hands of my father and mother
the hands of my grandfathers and
the hands of their grandmothers
appeared before me in the quick of a moment
passed over me in a flutter
leaving behind images of a bounty
whose fullness is clear
only in the absence of time.

Clasped within this moment—
tiny itself, yet capable of holding the swells
of time passed and time future—
was the stoop of Walter's back, fingers ruffling leaves
to find pods bursting with the sweetness of now,
and the bend of Charlotte's neck shucking sweet corn
to the cry of gulls and the murmur of women's voices;
was the fold of Guido's arm cradling basil-tinged tomatoes,
wrapping and passing them to family who dropped by the kitchen,
and the twist of metal on glass as Sally put up
the last of the pickled cukes for winter;
were the tendrils of time snaking out from these fruits to their sources:
backwards through the gates at Ellis Island to a time
somewhere before the cold waters circling Aland
somewhere before Calabria's warm clay

back to the hands of men and women
felt now only as whisper.

And, along the dense brim of this same moment,
time passing forward again,
whisper rising to crescendo in my mother's voice
asking me to help pick our supper.
How I sighed with the burden
of getting off the couch to gather;
how only fleetingly, barely consciously
I wondered at the sweetness of our meal
and then moved on to the dire press
of whatever childish circumstance
I was living through.
Not noticing how it was I was living at all.
Not noticing the back and arms that cleared
the trees and stones to make way for dirt.
Not noticing the hands that sprinkled seed.
Not noticing the mind full of the land,
ready to tip out its secrets only for the asking.

Indeed, it wasn't until one came after me
that I understood what making generations meant.
That I understood the gifts of the land gathered by my father and his father,
men who refused to forget the feel of dirt on their fingers
long past the time of necessity.
That I understood how this gift was bound to those others:
of presence, of nurture, of commitment that marked my growing,
and that would be my wellspring for all my time.

And so it is that, stooping before the seed pods
from lilies finished for the season,
I think long before clipping:
think of a beauty found only in the excess of luxury
permitted me by the work of those who came before;
think of those who struggled to make our generations survive;
think of those who will come after who will not know firsthand
the bounty of my father's hands or his father's hands
or even of my own, but who will carry in their hands
a bodily memory, the fullness of time witnessed in their gathering of fruit.

Last Visit

BY JADENE FELINA STEVENS

Its cloying scent by the door
prompts my mother to comment
... *that's a Tree of Heaven* ...

I know this, not that the tree
is sent from heaven, but that
my mother must excuse

its intrusion as we pass in
or out of the rooming house
which she insists is *home.*

The landlord no longer sprays
the premises periodically
and the closet rustles

a noise like crepe rubbing together
or leaves in a faint wind, cockroaches
invade her boxes, her clothes

so that now, whatever she must wear
she drapes over the straightbacked chair
... *a waterbug* ... she says

as one crosses the floor, as though
she has to excuse it, excuse her life
as though to rename the ugly

will transform it. I nod, ask her to come
with me. She smiles, shakes her head
kisses me, lights another cigarette.

Questions

MARY DOERING

mother, mother my dreams
are filled with your sighs
they cross state lines
enter my heart
where they sit at a long rectangular table
hands folded, ankles crossed, back straight

were you playing dead
resigned to working the crossword puzzle
the yellow pencil filled with regret
while I waited, impatient to interrupt
watching you cheat
looking up the answers in the back

why did you destroy the records
perhaps it is just as well
you watched me leave
the back door screen
forming a veil
over your small thin face

when did you loose the ability
to take down life's dictation
snagged in the web of depression
folding in and in
repeating   I shall not want
I shall not want

The Right Place

BY JEBBA M. HANDLEY

ABOVE ALL THINGS, BOOKS WERE what my mother and I shared best. Deeply. Lovingly. Packages of books went back and forth between us, even when I lived in Greece. We were immune to book-rate. Postage be damned. We discussed them lengthily, by phone and letter, in penetrating terms; the motives, the relationships, the vocabulary, the style. In the guise of sharing literary characters we no doubt revealed a great deal about ourselves. I shouldn't have been surprised then, when my mother told me she was making a great change in her life.

It was thirty-five years ago when my mother retired from her life in New York City and settled in Lincolnville, Maine, a brave thing to do at sixty. I couldn't believe she would be happy leaving her city life, and all its excitements, its museums, its concerts, its theater and its restaurants. She purchased a sweet, simple farm house with a beautiful barn where she could live with a friend and carry on her career as a sculptor. The thing that took my breath away on first visiting her was the killer view from the kitchen window—five acres of meadow down to Penobscott Bay, bordered on either side by stands of pine. That vista nourished my mother for twenty years, but so did the community in which she found herself. It was filled with artists, teachers, writers, and singers, many of them world-renowned. She settled in and found a circle of friends with whom she had as much in common as she had in her life in New York.

As the years passed I rejoiced for her, but I was envious too, that she had landed in a place so nurturing of her talent and so welcoming in friendship. I grew secure in the knowledge that my mother resided in a community of friends who cared about each other, who would come to her as quickly in a night emergency as they would in the day with a basket of bounty from their gardens. I yearned for the time that might happen to me. And then it did.

Life, just like a storm, lifted me up, tossed me about, blew me to various cities and then deposited me in Chatham. My husband and I had been off-season weekenders and Christmas vacationers here for years, but we were outsiders to the community. We came here only to rest from our too-hectic lives in Connecticut. Then suddenly in '92 my husband was offered early retirement, and we arrived in a town we didn't really know.

A nor'easter was hurling itself about the town, bringing in rain at a slant as I hurried into a gourmet food store in Chatham. The place was crowded with people enjoying soup and sandwiches at little tables. They were exchanging news with the owner who went from table to table. I ordered chowder, and, as if I were a guest in her living room, the owner welcomed me and introduced me to some of the lunchtime diners seeking refuge from the rain. It's funny how a storm can bring intimacy to total strangers, as if we were leaves blown one upon the other, then lodged by the wind against a doorstep.

I was bent over my soup when the door banged open sending a gust of wind swirling about the store. "Oh, what a day," the new customer said. A crash of lightning rent the sky, then plunged the shop and all the other shops in the complex into darkness. "Ooohh, don't you love a good storm?" said the voice in the dark. The lights came on in a couple of minutes and suddenly some of the other customers began telling tales of great storms on the Cape. I sat spooning my soup, listening, and felt a calmness inside me I hadn't known for years.

The owner of the food store became my first friend. Through her I met others and took steps—like the Lippizzaners' *passage*, those hesitating, almost syncopated, breathless steps, into the life of the town. My town.

Since then, I've often thought about the similarity of our choices: my mother's in Maine, mine in Chatham, our coastal epiphanies, our need for the comfort and substance of rock, pine trees and sea. The necessity we share for a vibrant community of doers, people who actively pursue their talents, who, in sharing them, make it a richer place for all. I'm interested in the risks we took to make such changes. The courage and the willingness to fail.

My mother went to a town in which she knew no one. There, in her white clapboard house, and her big barn filled with stone from quarries and Maine beaches, her hammers and chisels, she built a new life, making friends and sharing her abilities. Famous for her portrayal of animals in wood or stone, she spent two summers carving the famous seal, André, a larger-than-life portrait in granite of this much beloved animal. When it was done, she gave it to the townspeople of Rockport for their park by the harbor. It was her way of expressing gratitude for her life in Maine.

As she found her place along the shores of Penobscott Bay, I came to a light-filled house in Chatham, the first I'd ever owned. Our road leads in through the woods to a driveway of clam shells which sing our coming with their welcoming crunch. I awake to the music of cardinals. I work as a writer, now and then gazing out my studio window to three enormous spruces I call "my girls." I feel included in the chatter of the resident crows in my forest and I dine on gifts from the sea, fresh clams and oysters, bluefish and cod. I fall asleep to the lullaby of waves when the wind blows through the open window from the east.

I have found peace and nourishment in my surroundings. I'm the lucky giver and receiver in a community of friends. I, like my mother, have landed in a perfect place. I could not ask for more.

Motherhood

BY JUDITH PARTELOW

Under a long cotton nightgown
  We have swept away a thousand nights
  pinning a sap-sucking honey bee
  against a naked thorn.

Women with cool ankles leap across doorways
  and bend above the cribs of time
  to dribble blue ink inside a hollow well.

Moistened fingers clinging to our hair
  play a fiddle-tune
  an endless tune
  we dance to all our lives.

EDITH VONNEGUT, "RIP TIDE," OIL ON CANVAS

Pasta Della Nonna

BY VIRGINIA REISER

"EAT, EAT," MY NONNA SAID. "You are like cappellini—too thin to hold a sauce."

My grandmother worshiped at the altar of food. For years I had avoided her fingers as they prodded my waist, and then her prayers to eat more. I had even avoided visiting. Her kitchen was a simmering stew of unwholesome smells unlike my friends' homes. Their mothers popped little frozen trays into ovens and peeled back foil to expose perfect compartments of food groups. Instead, Nonna peeled root vegetables, crossed herself religiously, and called on an unhearing God to make me fatter.

Nonna had lived in America for over 50 years and never seemed to learn. For one thing, she kept chickens. Many times my father laughed and told how the chickens, with their scent of the earth city people had left behind, made the neighbors nervous. More than one had called the animal officer. When she saw the dark blue van drive up, Nonna was ready. "Please come in," she said. "I hope you can help me." Confectioners' sugar dusted her left cheek and sprinkled over the top of her gray sweater. On her arm she balanced a plate of two towers of pastries—one of tiny hats filled with apricot jam, the other twisted branches of sugar and butter.

"The ladies in my church group are coming over. They are all such good cooks. I cannot shame myself. Which of these tastes better?" A trail of sugar fell on the carpet and across the officer's uniform. Before he knew it, he was drinking small dark coffees at Nonna's kitchen table and she was demonstrating her favorite tomato sauce. Sliced onions dropped in sizzling olive oil, their sides jumping in anticipation of the garlic to come. Then she got out the special rolling pin she had brought from Italy. "Fresh eggs always make the best pasta," she said.

Over the years, some of the officers came back and brought their sweethearts or wives to watch Nonna make pasta. She sniffed at their perfume and wondered how they could catch a man smelling like dead carnations instead of aged Parmesan.

Each time my father finished this story, I smiled. But inside, where my heart stood apart in a cage of bone, I agreed with the neighbors. Nonna was an embarrassment.

Now she pulled my nose into a platter of broad, long noodles splattered with a ragu rich with beef, marrow, tomatoes, butter, cream, and nutmeg. "If you are afraid to eat, you are afraid to live. No wonder that man left you." I tried to think of the last time I had eaten butter. It was easier than remembering the day Dan had left. His note said only, "I am moving to a different apartment. I think you will find everything in order." The counters were clean; the spice bottles were alphabetical, their contents evenly balanced. Even the spoons were lined up in the drawer, bowls cradled together perfectly. I sat on the kitchen floor and blamed the past.

The pasta's steam rolled over my face. My pores seemed to widen and I could feel my hair straighten and flatten at the temples. I pushed the platter away. "Nonna, it does smell delicious, but I'm not hungry."

She pushed the plate back in my face. "All morning I have cooked for you," she cried. She crossed herself three times and called upon the saints to look at the granddaughter who dishonored her. "At five, I gather the eggs. At seven, I start the sauce. I chop, I stir, I simmer for five, six, seven hours. Then, and only then, do I make the pasta. I knead. I roll, I roll, I roll until the pasta is so thin you can see God through it. And then she says to me, 'I am not hungry.' "

"I'm sorry, Nonna."

"The angels are crying to me, Rosemaria, because they do not have stomachs and cannot eat my pasta. And you say you are sorry. Can you give me back my morning, my afternoon? What is wrong with you? Eat." The platter was inching its way towards me again. Now the steam was sending up only occasional puffs like a peace pipe passed among once-warring tribes. Two more crosses and an imprecation and it was in my mouth.

Nonna's arms relaxed. She lined up the salt and pepper shakers on the old pine table. She was careful to avoid the slope caused by the weight of her arms after years of coaxing dough into pasta. She marched the shakers behind the oil and vinegar cruets and the toothpick cup. "Well, well? How is it? Too rich? Too much nutmeg? The pasta—it was warm today. I worried."

I tried hard to find a fault, but I couldn't. I had forgotten the sense of butter as it binds a sauce. It coated the pasta and the mouth like a kiss. The noodles were slippery like fresh oysters. The bits of braised beef were so tender they were as one with the tomatoes.

"It's perfect, Nonna." Only then did she help herself.

"Yes, it is good," she said. She looked towards the ceiling above my head and sighed. "Rosemaria, I want you to stay with me for the weekend. I am an old lady now and my legs are not working so good as before. Unless you are too busy now that that man is gone."

She saw the protest in my eyes and, between bites of pasta, began calling on Mary to give her strength.

There was no reason to deny her. There was every reason to believe Dan would never return. I had found a statue of St. Francis in a thrift store. I had pasted a canning label across his knotted belt, saying "St. Anthony." I had hung rosary beads around his neck and lit a blue votive candle. Each morning and night, I prayed to the saint of the lost. Dust filmed over the statue's halo, but Dan never called. I bought new spoons and put them in a separate drawer. I never used the ones Dan had arranged so carefully. My soul seemed to be trapped in those cupped bowls, nestled so intimately together. I was upside down and I did not know how to turn the spoons to make everything rightside-up.

"All right, Nonna. I'll be here Saturday before noon."

"No, Rosemaria. Come Friday night. I'll need help with the chickens Saturday morning."

Before she could call on another saint, I agreed.

Friday night, the kitchen smelled of garlic and summer. Nonna made chicken with olives and potatoes with rosemary. I knew the chicken was one of Nonna's own, its neck twisted with hands strong from kneading. I felt my stomach tighten.

"Rosemaria, what is wrong with you? Do you think God gave us chickens to pet like dogs? Should I let their legs get old like mine and take them to a veterinarian to be put out of their misery? Is it not true, when we eat the egg, we eat the chicken? Sometimes it is good to put one chicken to rest and watch the others strengthen." She watched as I pierced a thigh with a wavering fork. "If you approach your world like this, you will always be afraid." She put her hand over mine and pushed the fork down quickly. I had to admit, the chicken was the best I had ever tasted.

The next morning, she woke me at five. The chickens were fluttering in their roost, but they knew Nonna's step and why she had come. The sky was just beginning to streak with morning.

"Look at that," said Nonna. "Just like a good prosciutto. It will be a fine day. Here, sprinkle the seed around you and they will come. I will find the eggs."

The seed felt as heavy as the sleep in my eyes. I scattered it in clouds around me. The chickens hustled out, clucking, the rooster first. Their eyes never looked directly—they always seemed to be angling off. But they found the seed and pawed the ground with twigged feet.

Nonna came out of the roost. Her eyes shone. "Look, four eggs." She cradled them into her apron pockets where her body would keep them warm and safe. "Fresh eggs make the best pasta," she said, "and warm eggs make the pasta even better. You will see."

I followed her into the kitchen and opened a cupboard door. The linoleum rubbed the earth from between my toes. "Rosemaria, what are you looking for?"

"Herb tea, Nonna."

"Herb tea? Herb tea? How can you drink grass in the morning. I know you cannot be a cow because you are too thin, but are you a goat? On such a morning as this, you must be alive to the possibilities. Here, drink this coffee."

It was too early for the litany of saints, so I took the coffee and braced myself for the day to come. I realized I had forgotten my morning prayer to St. Anthony and silently asked for forgiveness.

"Don't bend your head like that, Rosemaria. It makes your chin double. Try always to keep your face up. That is why the saints are in heaven." Nonna stood drinking her coffee against the counter. The sunrise was furious now, shooting red and yellow across the room and over her face. The eggs bulged in her pockets and she put her cup down to caress them. I raised my head to feel the sun's heat on my face.

"Look, how pretty," Nonna said. "Your face is all rosy, like ground beef before it is browned."

Dan had always said I wasn't beautiful, but attractive for my type. When I asked him what my type was, he said, "You know . . . the sensitive kind." When I demanded more details, he said, "You're being too sensitive."

"Go change," Nonna said gently. "Today we make the ravioli; first the filling, then the sauce, and then the pasta." She rolled the eggs in her pockets like a gambler rolling dice.

An apron enclosed my waist like two arms. Had Dan fit around me like this? I watched Nonna work. She cubed pork and leftover chicken into tiny pieces. She browned the pork in a little butter until it looked like dark spangles on a foamy gown. She showed me the green bitter vein in a chicken liver and how to pull it out as if it were a thread coming from a needle. Into the pan it went and quickly plumped.

"Never overcook the liver, Rosemaria. Always keep it so it still feels alive under your finger or it will be tough." She took my finger and put it on the liver. It felt firm on the sides, but I could feel its center move under my touch. She took the liver out of the pan, diced it, and set it aside. Now the chicken, diced onions, garlic and chopped rosemary were crowding the pork in the pan. Nonna stirred and I started to feel hungry. A little grated orange zest, salt, pepper, and then some wine and cream. The filling bubbled and thickened. She turned off the heat and added the liver and some grated Parmesan.

"Now is the most important part, Rosemaria. You must taste. We cook to eat, we eat to live, but we taste to love."

The smell of the filling made my mouth water. Nonna put a spoonful near my face. I blew the steam in her direction and took the filling in my mouth. I rolled it around and felt it with my tongue. I swallowed. "I think it needs some salt."

"Some salt?" Her spoon danced from her hip to wave in front of my face. "When you are marching with the angels in the desert, then you need to taste more salt." She tasted. "Rosemaria, today Our Lady is smiling. I am proud of you. You are right." She raised her spoon in salute.

She anointed the filling with some salt, tasted again, and made a simple sauce of butter, diced prosciutto, and reduced cream. Dan would have been frightened of such a sauce. A vegetable steamer and low-fat dressing were as important to him as sit-ups and a daily run. The first three months, I had gotten up to run with him, but he was always a block ahead. The next month, I ran every other day, and finally, not at all.

Nonna took the eggs out of her pockets. She smiled and held one up to the light. I could see the sun piercing through the vapors of garlic and butter that hung in the air. I draped a strand of my hair under my nose. It felt slick and smelled of rosemary. Nonna blessed herself. "Now, the pasta. You and I will each make some, Rosemaria. Watch me close and do as I do."

She poured two mounds of flour directly on each end of the pine table. She dug a well in one and motioned for me to do the same. She cracked each of her two eggs in one hand and opened them with the same hand. The yolks spilled out into the hole in the flour. When I tried, the yolks broke and stretched around jagged pieces of shell I had left behind.

I heard her call on my own St. Anthony as she raised her eyes. "Please let Rosemaria find all the shells she has lost or the pasta, it will be biting back when we eat it."

Nonna used her fingers to beat the eggs in their well. She took her forefinger and made the round larger and larger as she incorporated more flour into the center. Her eggs never crossed the flour wall or tumbled over it. My own walls had been violated and the eggs were escaping into a moat on the outside of the flour. Soon they would be a barge of ooze falling off the table. Nonna rushed over to stop the dam with floured hands. "There you see. A little flour in the right place and all is not lost."

Finally, she began to knead. My hands were encased in mittens of flour and eggs. I picked up my dough ball and threw it down on the table.

"Rosemaria, what are you doing? Has this dough done something bad to you that you must spank it? You must use strength, yes, but gentle strength. Do not let the dough know your anger or it will always snap back at you. It will harden and taste of bitterness."

I could feel the tears gather across my eyes. I only hoped they wouldn't muster and march across my face. "But, Nonna, it's only dough."

"No, Rosemaria, it is food. Food is to nourish, to nurture. When we do not care about what we eat, we do not care about how we live. And then, I don't know what will become of us."

We both kneaded. As we pushed and pulled, the rhythm of the dough and the kisses it gave the table became soothing. The dough seemed to sigh and relax as it became smooth and warm.

"Now the dough must take a rest and become itself. Let us have another coffee and then we will roll the pasta for the ravioli."

She drank her coffee and told me of Italy and the sauce of her mother. It was a complicated procedure: many organ meats and spices, slow braising, and long cooking in a special pot placed in wood embers in the corner of a fireplace. "To taste this sauce on mama's pasta, it was to walk with St. Peter on water and never get your feet wet, and to feel the breath of angels on your cheeks," Nonna said. "Any man who tasted this sauce fell in love with mama on the spot. One day, the padre came and asked to speak to mama privately. She never made the sauce again. I remember this sauce when I was very little. Mama would never tell me everything that was in it. But I had many proposals."

Dan never would have loved me for such a sauce. He preferred to cook our meals himself. "You make such a mess," he'd say.

Nonna prodded the dough as if it were a relic from a favorite saint. She took out the special pin for rolling pasta that she had brought with her from Italy. It was narrow, long, and tapered at both ends. It was smooth with the years of her palms.

"Stand back, Rosemaria. Leave room for the saints to help." She rolled the dough and within seconds it seemed to cover half the table. She rolled it over itself onto the pin and with her hands feathered it from the center of the pin to the outsides. She unrolled the pasta, turned it, and gathered it all around the pin again. The dough stretched and thinned, "For the ravioli, we do not want to see the world through the dough. No, we want it to be like Our Lord's shroud in Torino, able to cover the ravioli, but still make its own impression. You try."

Handling the dough on the pin, I thought my hands were like oxen standing on a tissue. The more I tried, the more holes I pushed through the dough. "I can't do it, Nonna."

"Yes, you can, Rosemaria." She put her hands over mine. They were warm, the fingers thick, yet papered with age. The pasta formed slowly as we stretched together. It didn't look as supple as Nonna's, but it was done.

We cut the pasta into strips and filled it. The ravioli looked like little cushions as they sat on platters next to the stove. Nonna put a pot of water on to boil and heated the cream sauce.

"It's time to eat the pasta," she said. There were enough ravioli for six people, but Nonna and I ate them all. They slipped into our mouths, one after the other. They tasted of the work of morning and the promise of evening. We drank Chianti and played gin. Nonna won by calling on St. Theresa to find out what I was saving.

When I got ready to leave the next morning, Nonna handed me the pasta pin. "You must take this, Rosemaria," she said. "Our Lady came to me in a dream and told me that she wants you to have it. I will be gone soon and when Jesus comes down again, she wants to be sure he will get something decent to eat. Besides, Aunt Ursula can send me another one."

"Thank you, Nonna." I cradled the pin in my arms. Her hands had worn it as smooth as satin. "I will try to make the pasta as well as you do."

"Then, take these eggs from the chickens today." She pulled out three eggs from her pockets. They were warm from her body. "Be sure you come by each week and get some more eggs. Fresh eggs make the best pasta."

When I got home, I put the eggs on the counter and the pasta pin in the corner. I ran to the bedroom, but there was still no message from Dan. I lay down on the bed and composed another prayer. I looked at St. Anthony, got up, and tore off the label. I wondered how St. Francis, the patron saint of animals, felt about chickens. I went into the kitchen and opened the drawer with the spoons Dan had arranged. I picked them up and threw them in the garbage. I put the eggs in my pockets and the pin on the table. Then I went back out to buy some flour.

Growing Up

BY CELIA BROWN

for Michael at 17

I no longer had to stand on chairs
to find the pot or jar that I hid
from myself on high.
A long-armed child reached up,
grabbed it easily.
I was reminded of giraffes in the forest
and the moose I once saw nibbling
In downtown Alaska.
Even the rubber tree I planted
ten years ago had taken over the house.
Everything grew up but me.

DRAWING BY RHODA M. STALEY

JEANNIE MOTHERWELL, "EYES LOOK TAKE A LOOK," COLLAGE, 1999

III

On Love and Other Ties that Bind

Acme Coin-A-Wash

BY KRISTIN KNOWLES

I recline on a weathered bench
in the breezeway of the laundromat,
my drip dry garments strewn across car doors wide-open.
The colorless woman in the Ford Taurus sedan
does not address me directly
but audibly mutters under her breath,
emoting the tension of too many sunny days spent indoors,
martyred arms sorting lights and darks
until everything becomes a rhythmic gray redundancy.
I focus on the hypnotic hum of dryers spinning,
percussion provided by a pair of sneakers.
Moist and radiant,
the clothes dance with wild abandon,
aware that they, at any moment,
will be borne into a new day's incarnation.
August afternoons are like this:
lazy, seductive, sleepy warmth . . .
reflective and ripe with romance.

A robust baritone drifts out the back door
of Rosina's kitchen during the lunch rush,
a spicy Italian operetta,
floating over the dumpster,
across the lifeless parking lot
and into my contemplation.
I remember a sultry July moonrise
when you tended the fire while I crushed the garlic:
plump, golden, pungent . . .
my fingertips fragrant with flavor.
You called me outside to show me the moon
and I leaned back into your frame,
savoring the summer musk of your skin
and thinking I had never known such comfort.

Red wine and outdoor fires,
late nights giving way to sunrise,
clad only in the folds of too-long unwashed sheets
as the bedroom curtains witnessed
our sacred ritual.
The inviting friction of beach sand
inspired further tactile pursuits
until our burnished bare feet slept entangled.
Yeah, this is another poem about summer love
so you don't need to know how it ended . . .
How we make history is as incidental as our crossing paths.

As the Ford Taurus is replaced by a minivan
I am returned to my mundane laundromat moment.
I notice that the washing machines have ceased their chatter
and the hum of the dryers has dimmed,
dissipating into the afternoon shadows, solemnly cast,
pensive, dark and sweet.
Perhaps, my passing lover,
the cycle is complete.

CONNIE BLACK, "HERE WE GO ROUND," MONOPRINT

Anthology

BY JUDITH PARTELOW

I keep jars of multi-colored glass
   found on scattered beaches where I walk,
a collection of colors
   the gathering of which
   joins the jagged edges of the past
and holds them safely in a bottle on my shelf.

Pieces of pottery intrigue me most:
broken cups and saucers, dishes and tureens,
the wares of women spilling off the waves,
faded patterns of a woman's dreams—
the crockery seized and smashed
that once was filled, then washed and wiped
and gently placed upon the board.

LINDA MCCAUSLAND, PHOTOGRAPH

The House of my Birth

BY ELEANOR FERRI JONES

ISOLATED AND ALONE, THE HOUSE LOOKED OUT onto sprawling mud flats and marshy grass that edged the tidal creek. Sometimes the sea would seep in gently, evening the surface irregularities of the surrounding land and making one giant puddle that almost, but never quite, reached the front steps. Not the angry destructive force of the Atlantic that viciously attacked the rocky shore only half a mile away—no, it was a calm, silent flooding that made a miniature pond where the back yard sloped down into a deep gully.

The house itself was old; we never did find the record of its origin. "Built when Christ wore short pants," my father would venture irreverently. We heard stories that it had first been a small yacht club, then moved away from the water and converted to a residence. Many additions must have been made over the years—each one a haphazard extension of the main building. First a room in front, then another at the back, eventually gables sprouted out of the attic, creating an upstairs floor of tiny cubicles with steeply slanted walls. This awkward cluster of rooms lent themselves very well to the variety of assignments allocated to them. There were times when we all lived upstairs, and downstairs became a source of income. During affluent years we used the whole house ourselves. Sometimes the living room was at the back, sometimes it was the one in front. Sometimes we enjoyed the luxury of a parlor and a living room as well as a separate one for dining. It seemed that at one period or another almost every room took a turn as a bedroom, all except the kitchen and bathrooms which were never converted, probably only because of the inconvenience of rearranging the plumbing connections.

It was truly a monstrosity of a house, and the most impossible area of it all was the cellar. Sitting about four feet below the level of the ground outside, walls of fieldstone loosely assembled and held together with crumbling old cement, it was powerless to hold back the water from rain-soaked earth. It could only strain out the dirt, allowing the water—salty and fresh mixed together—to rise inexorably and quietly, a foot, often two feet deep. Somebody—I think it must have been my grandfather because he was a stonemason—had the inspiration to solve the problem by adding a layer of crushed stone on the cellar floor and topping it with a few inches of cement. This subtracted about nine inches of potential flooding area, but because it raised the floor by that distance, it also dropped the already too-low ceiling height the same number of inches. Fortunately, my grandparents, with whom we lived, as well as my parents, were rather short people, and when we were children it presented no great hardship for us. But as we grew taller, maneuvering became more difficult. And of course the water still found its way in. We did have a siphoning arrangement to assist in its removal: something that was screwed onto a faucet with two hoses attached, one sitting in the soapstone setup below and the other immersed in the water on the floor. For the life of me I could never understand how one got rid of unwanted water by running more in—but it did work—usually. However, when conditions outside were really bad, the tub filled with water that refused to drain, so it was necessary to turn off the faucet, pray that the tub wouldn't overflow and wait, like Noah, for the flood to subside. It was also necessary to refrain from flushing the upstairs toilet.

When that glorious day came that electricity replaced the old gas fixtures, another solution became a reality. Now we could have a pump set into a hole in the corner of the basement floor that would start miraculously when water reached the magic level. It would hum merrily, sucking up the unwanted intruder with gusto and expelling it noisily through a hole in the window above. This worked pretty well as long as the water level in the ground outside didn't come too near to the surface. When that occurred, and it happened occasionally, the water kept coming back in and the pump worked as hard as it could to keep up and, if we were fortunate, the race was sort of a tie.

As a child I needed to be involved in the "monster house" only in a minor way, but years later, when wartime demands took precedence over family obligations and I was compelled to relinquish my husband to Uncle Sam for the duration, I moved back with my new baby to the house of my birth, occupying the downstairs apartment which happened to be conveniently vacant. My parents and elderly grandmother lived upstairs. Now I was in full charge of dealing with the demon.

By this time, the encroachment of the sea had been controlled by dikes that stemmed the tidal floods, but the popularity of the New American toy, the automobile, and the spurt in suburban growth brought pavement to the streets, cement to the sidewalks and hot-topped tennis courts across the way. Surface water poured into the bare earth that remained and our battle with the flooding cellar continued—but thanks to our ally, the trusty pump, cellar remained mostly dry.

I will never forget that winter of '44—snowfall after gentle snowfall, and then the blizzard—two days of thick white flakes whirling into monumental drifts. Impossible to dig out the car—enough to keep open the narrow path to the street. Each shoveling built up the sides higher and higher until the walk was a white tunnel and there was no place to put the new snow. Inside we managed to keep warm—the snow that collected against walls and windows insulated against the wind outside. The furnace kept radiators comfortably hot. The coal bin was filled with more than enough fuel to finish out the worst of winters; good hard blue coal—my family prided on buying the best. I felt snug and safe in my "manless" home with my little son.

Then came the sudden thaw and pelting rain. All day Wednesday a steady downpour. All night and again Thursday there seemed no end to the leak in the heavens. From a glistening fairyland of virgin white, the world outside turned into an ice floe distorted by the shimmer of water pouring down a window pane.

Almost hourly I would open the door to the basement and listen for the reassuring hum of the pump, descending the stairs apprehensively to take a look at the water level in the well. When it was time to tend the furnace fire Thursday night ,I noticed the puddle in the coal bin—now I wouldn't be able to use the wet coal at the bottom. Pushing a shovel along a flat surface under a mound of stone and then pulling it away full is a comparatively simple operation, but trying to pierce the middle of a pile of choice blue anthracite was another story. The gentle, tentative nudging of the shovel against a row of coals might yield three or four pieces—an energetic swing into the pile could penetrate a couple of inches and get you a shovelful—but more likely a large hunk would jerk the shovel to a quick halt, splattering the rest of the heap. To add to the frustration, the bin was situated at the edge of the cellar furthest removed from the furnace— at least fifteen feet away. Each patiently filled shovelful had to be carried gingerly while ducking the low beams as well as heating and gas pipes that crossed the ceiling in every direction.

I finally banked the fire, persuaded myself that there was nothing to worry about—the coal bin often seeped water—it would just be a little inconvenient to avoid using the wet coals.

Friday morning it was still raining hard when I awoke. Jumping quickly out of bed, I ran to the cellar door, opened it uneasily. The familiar musty odor of old damp wet walls and the chill draft of moisture-laden air verified the sparkle of reflected light on the floor below. The faithful old pump was still chugging away, but it was obviously a losing fight. I donned my father's knee boots and descended the stairs to repair the havoc of debris floating in three or four inches of water.

What a mess! Tending the furnace was really tricky now. The coal pile fortunately was a fairly high pyramid, but a splatter of coal meant a splash of dirty water. It was comforting to feel the warmth of the glowing embers as I added more fuel—and I was positive that the fire bed was safely above any level the water might reach. When I went to adjust the damper an hour later, I began to lose some of my confidence—the water was rising steadily—now it was halfway up to the top of my boots and I had to walk slowly and deliberately, or the water would make waves that sometimes lapped over the edge of my boot and I knew the startle of icy water tickling down my calf and settling under my toes.

Then it happened—the faithful, dependable, invincible pump stopped running— suddenly, abruptly. No complaining whimper, not even a dying gash—nothing, just silence—sickening, terrifying silence. I felt impotent, alone, helpless—a cripple torn cruelly away from her crutch. Dampness had already penetrated the floor above; heat from the radiators did not completely absorb the chill of icy water below. And if the level of the water rose enough to put out the fire in the furnace, we would be in real trouble indeed— water against red hot metal could crack the heater.

I telephoned an SOS to the Fire Department. Our plight was common. Their list was so long they could make no promises. There were only two pumps in their stock of equipment and they were being used day and night all over the city. I bathed my baby quickly, wrapped him warmly, deposited him in the loving arms of his grandmother, and resumed my basement vigil. The water was coming in fast now that the pump had succumbed. I imagined I could see it rise visibly. When I next descended to add coal, it was within an inch from the top of my boots. I had to move very, very slowly. Getting a shovel of coal was an exercise in patience. Carefully I pushed the shovel in—two pieces of coal separated from the pile onto my shovel, another push to acquire more and they all slipped off, splashing into the water, sprinkling me with an icy spray. Angrily I swung the shovel hard into the pile and was lucky this time to half fill it, but in the effort bent my right knee forward just enough to allow the water to pour into my boot, running in to the very top. With one leg still relatively dry, I started the fifteen-foot trek to the furnace, unlatched the narrow door, opening it wide. I stepped back, aimed carefully and swung the shovel through the narrow aperture towards the bed of live coals. The tip of the shovel connected sharply with the top edge of the opening, almost throwing me off balance with the unexpected jolt and spewing the coals in every direction. Splash! Splash! Splash!

Freezing cold, clothing soaked and stained, I stood there, silently repeating all the swear words I had ever known.

It was then that I noticed it—a flicker of light shining through the mud and grime on the cellar window, a tiny patch of glistening sunlight. Suddenly I realized the rain had stopped. Hopelessness and despair melted into overwhelming relief. An hour later, the fire truck arrived—its powerful suction drained us dry in minutes, and somehow the pump was made to work once more. Life was joyous again!

KAREN GUNDERSON, "CAPE VISIT," OIL/PHOTOGRAPH, 1996

Saturdays

BY LINDA TURNER

Sorting through stacks of used lovers
(how dare we glare at each other!)
yours-mine, his-hers, identical resumes
interchangeable parts,
nameless, faceless,
categorized by whim.
Which is the prize, which deadly?
They seem so much the same.
The game is endless—
Roulette with the fiery wheels
of chariots drawn by four horsemen,
apocalyptic satyrs, bachelors one through four
While you listen for the sirens
blaring loudest near the reefs.
Flowing tresses tangle, gill-netting mortal men like you.
We are facing, what?
A challenge?
Did I/you dare you/me to be here?
And why, friend, why
are you the only man with a face I recognize?

Guerrilla sin Corazón

BY RENA LINDSTROM

Ay, revolucionario, I warn you,
You flee with my heart on your back,
ruby-globed contraband chucked in your pack
ticking like a handmade bomb
that could blow a careless man to Heaven.
You think you can overthrow love?
Not so easy, *campanero.*
It took us lives to meet again
histories lousy with war.
You think you can turn back safely,
now that you've undone me,
shattered the bony cage
with your tender sniper's aim,
loosed the archaic rhythm
into the blue narcotic night?
Now I'm bloody dangerous, *mi fugitivo querido.*
You might as well surrender.

Siren

BY JUDITH PARTELOW

Cold droplets bead across my brow
in jeweled formation.
Heat.
Unseen blankets cover me.
Dry, moistless sucking in of air,
my fan cannot redeem me.

I shall associate our meeting
with these first heavy breaths
of heated summer-longing:
a touch of chill to cool
my sweating arms
my open thighs
my sultry swaying walk
my furtive, beckoning eyes.

June is heavy with her burgeoning summer-child.
When she delivers
these days of languid tension,
she will deliver us all
from temptation.

Queen of the Ball

BY BARBARA STEPHENS

I'M NOT SUPPOSED TO LIKE COOKING. It's been my trademark for 36 years. My friends know it, and politely tell me to bring the soda or the chips when I'm invited to a party. I've also been in charge of ice. I especially like that job.

My mother loved to cook. Dinner was always a treat. She wasn't a Betty Crocker cook, making bread shaped in a knot or three-layered cakes. No, my mom was a Casserole Queen, throwing ingredients together, lathering it all up with some Campbell's cream of mushroom soup. And none of us kids were ever allowed in the kitchen to help her cook. As a homemaker, it was her role. Our entrance would have diminished it, and I gladly obliged.

But now that I'm older, things have begun to change. It started small, a simple appetizer. I was invited to a party where I didn't know many people. I wanted to make a good impression, so I called my mom for an easy recipe, stressing the word easy. The infamous Pineapple Cheeseball was born. The ingredients appalled me, but she assured it was a crowd-pleaser. Trusting her expertise, I dipped my hands into the mess of cream cheese, pineapple chunks, green peppers, onions and pecans, "smushing" it all together. "Roll it into two balls" she had informed me. As I lifted each sticky finger out of the semi-solid goo, my brow furrowed in frustration. Rolling was impossible; I must have done it wrong. Confirmation—I am not a cook.

With cream cheese oozing between my fingers, I carefully picked up the phone and dialed that familiar number. Mom's Texas drawl tap-danced across the phone line. "You don't really roll it, honey. Just press it together into a ball." I should have known there was something missing in the instructions, especially coming from a Southern casserole cook. So I squeezed the sticky mess into two oddly shaped balls, complaining constantly that it looked more like thick soup than a soft cheeseball. That's when she added another piece of missing advice. "It's really better if you make it a day ahead and then let it sit in the fridge to harden." Since the party was in two hours, that plan was scratched. I slapped one cheeseball on a silver plate with crackers and ran out the door.

The Pineapple Cheeseball was a grand success, and overnight I became the Pineapple Cheeseball Queen. Wherever I went, it followed and everyone paid homage.

But it was hard to live up to the expectations of the Pineapple Cheeseball. No longer could I get by with bringing the chips or ice. The exalted cheeseball was required for every gathering. Sometimes people chastised me if I didn't make it. I may have been a queen, but I was a queen in a rut.

Last summer I decided to branch out, to rise above the simple little appetizer, and go where few non-cooks have gone before: pie-baking! With determination, I called my mom again, asking for a blueberry pie recipe. I was going to change my title even if it killed me.

Excited by this prospect, I hand-picked the blueberries myself. I perused the baking aisle for the perfect pie crust. I smiled as I chose two graham cracker pie crusts, one for the top and one for the bottom. Bursting with homemaker joy, I rushed home with my treasures.

I stirred the blueberries in the sugar, relishing their freshness, watching them burst at the slightest touch. Proudly, I assembled them in the bottom pie crust. Remembering my mother's instructions on the execution of the top pie crust, I hesitated, thinking that something just wasn't quite right. Carefully, I flipped the tin foil base on top of the pie. When I removed it, the beautiful graham cracker crust resembled a jigsaw puzzle. Unable to live up to my baking expectations, I once again sought help from the Queen who had come before me.

With phone in hand, I gazed forlornly at the broken pieces. My mother answered, and the distress in my voice called out for her wisdom. She went into a long spiel of how difficult it is to manage the top pie crust. "Oh, now, sometimes it doesn't look pretty, but don't worry about it. Just press the dough together, and it'll be fine." "What dough?" I cried back. As I described my choice of pie crust, she burst into fits of laughter. "Pillsbury dough pie crust, the frozen kind, is what you need, honey," she explained between giggles. That's when I realized my pie crust debacle. My mom said, "Don't worry; they'll eat it anyway."

So we had blueberry cobbler instead, and they loved it, scooping up all the blueberries and crumbled crust. But I couldn't rejoice at my new Pie/Cobbler Queen status. They still wanted the Pineapple Cheeseball.

Mom makes excellent cheesecake. I figure that could be what knocks the Pineapple Cheeseball off hundreds of Cape Cod appetizer tables. At that point I'll have to admit that I'm a cook and worse . . . that I like it. But I'm not telling anyone yet, because sometimes it's just easier to bring the ice.

PINEAPPLE CHEESE BALLS

Mix together:
16 ounces of cream cheese, softened
1 8$^1/_2$ oz. can of crushed pineapple, drained
$^1/_4$ cup of chopped green peppers
2 tbsp. chopped onions
1 tsp. seasoned salt
2 cups of chopped pecans (1 cup of pecans for mix,
    1 cup for rolling of cheese balls
1 tsp. chives (optional)

Beat cream cheese until light and fluffy, stir in pineapple. Add green pepper, onion, seasoned salt, 1 cup pecans and chives: Mix well. Shape into 2 balls. Sprinkle with remaining pecans. Chill until firm.

Submitted by Lea Flowers, Pres.
Sigma Gamma No. 10465, Rolla, Missouri
The Golden Anniversary Cookbook, Beta Sigma Phi International
Press/Nashville EMS, 1980

Night Watch

BY MARY DOERING

Alone in the dark
watching red numbers
change
listening for the sound
of tires on gravel

bare feet touch cold floor
descend stair
walk through rooms
gray green with moonlight
everything in shadow

small light above the kitchen sink
casts a vague circle
back door still unlocked
crumpled lace table cloth
on the washing machine

stains from Christmas dinner
need special attention this year
the quarrel still stuck
in the threads
and in the woman

Sister Sally: Loved to Death

BY PAMELA CHATTERTON PURDY

January 20, 1997, 7:00 pm

MY BROTHER-IN-LAW GERRY was on the phone. Sally had once again undergone surgery at the Washington Hospital Center, Washington, D.C. Her condition was critical. She was losing her battle with colon cancer.

Sally was 58, Gerry considerably older. He had been a pilot during World War II, was shot down, survived a prison camp; and later became a corporate engineer. He was a problem solver and this was the toughest problem he had ever encountered.

He met me at the airport and in minutes we were at the hospital. We entered Sally's room. My heart sank. She lay there disoriented, eyes and mouth half open. She had undergone an eleven hour surgery which removed most of what was left of her organs. The salt level in her blood was 190 when 145 was considered high. Her blood pressure this morning had been 80/50; now it was 90/60. The chemical imbalance in her blood had caused stiffness in her arms and legs. Her tongue was curled in her mouth causing garbled speech. Tall and thin, a former Miss Rhode Island beauty queen, she moved about the bed constantly. She had an incredible sense of humor and after a prior surgery with a team of doctors examining her, she had exclaimed, "I feel like a God damned tossed salad."

Two months earlier I had stayed here by her bedside and once again a cot was being rolled in for me. I prepared for the long night. Sally's morphine was increased and I was assured she would sleep through the night. At about 4:00 pm, I insisted Gerry go and get some rest. He had kept a constant vigil for weeks now. I would see him in the morning.

Dawn came and I wondered if I had slept. Did I ever stop crying; crying and praying? "Surely He hath born our griefs and carried our transgressions." I had been married for thirty—four years to my husband David, a Methodist Minister. Words from scripture and hymns kept bounding through my mind.

Light was breaking through the curtains as the morning team of doctors walked in. They could see how distraught I was. I had to pause to overcome the lump in my throat.

"I just kept praying that she would slip away in the middle of the night," I whispered.

One of the doctors took me by the elbow and we went into the hall. The other doctors soon followed. They agreed that there was little that they could do. There was perceptible relief in their demeanor that a family member was expressing the wish to end the suffering. We would meet later that morning when Gerry arrived.

When Gerry walked in at 10:30, he could see by my face that all was not well. He agreed that it was futile to continue further treatment. There was sad resignation in his voice. He needed permission to give up the fight.

Doctors met us in the small conference room across the hall. We were told that the ileostomy had never really "kicked in"; that they could continue to tinker with her blood chemistry but that she inevitably would not make it. There was talk of letting Sally fly home to Atlanta to die, but the trip would surely be too much for her. She needed the twenty-four hour care she was receiving.

Gerry asked the difficult question, "How long until the end?"

"Seven to ten days," was the reply.

None of us spoke for a few moments; tears rolled steadily down my cheeks. My twisted heart was saying, "That long?" and at the same time. "So soon?"

Gerry and I went back toward Sally's room. Gerry stopped to call their eighteen-year-old daughter, Claire, at College. We knew that this would be the last hospital trip that she would have to make.

Nightfall and the Biblical rite of bathing and rubbing her wasted body continued. I would kiss her and help turn her. Every two hours the loving routine continued. By morning her blood pressure had improved to 105/65.

Gerry and I sat beside Sally in profound sadness. It rains on all, the just and the unjust, we agreed. Gerry clicked on the Australian Tennis Open and Sally began to focus. Tennis was one of Sally's passions, and even though we could barely understand her garbled speech, she would groan at a missed shot. I quietly nodded to Gerry that I was going to make some phone calls. I routinely called David, my mother and my twin sister Penelope, twice a day.

How do I protect Mom from yet another loss? Of four daughters, she was about to loose a second. My sister Phyllis had died at the age of thirty-three.

"Mom is a brick," Sally had always said. It was as if Sally was now coaching me in my thoughts. She adored Mom and always marveled at her backbone.

My conversation with Mom was brief. I assured her that Sally was resting comfortably, but not in very good shape. Through a strained voice, Mom asked me to buy Sally a long stemmed yellow rose. "Tell her I love her . . . I wish I could speak to her . . . I wish I were there . . ."

"Mom this time it is not your turn. At least I can spare you this much."

Sally's face brightened at the sight of the yellow rose. "This is from Mom Sally."

I knew I would be placing it in her hands after she died. Mom had asked the funeral director to place two white roses in Phyllis's hands before she was cremated.

I looked at Sally knowing her morphine would be increased and that the 3000 calorie I.V. when empty would not be replaced.

Around 2:00 pm, I left Sally and Gerry holding hands. They needed to be alone and I needed to find the chapel. I hoped she would be comfortable in her last days. There was that word again, hope. I guess I was not living without hope after all.

Gerry left about 4:30 pm after a two hour trip down memory lane. Both Gerry and Sally had been married before, but they had had twenty-one wonderful years together.

Early evening I made my calls. Mom's voice was garbled with grief as she repeated. "Tell her I love her . . . kiss her for me."

I assured Mom she was not suffering, that she was surrounded with love.

I had taken the time to call while the nurses bathed and tended to Sally. I walked in to see the full measure of what the cancer and efforts to save her life had left. She lay naked, probably weighing one hundred pounds. There was a scar from the center of her collar bone to her pubic bone. A four foot long tube came out of her stomach and descended to a bag of green bile. An ileostomy bag of secretions hung from her left side. Her rectum had been removed and her bottom had not healed. The bloody packing was being removed and changed. I was shocked to see a spider web of black marking on her torso; a target for her radiation.

This bodily horror traced her fight for life, her pure sacrifice of herself for her husband and daughter. She was the image of the Pieta, the suffering Christ.

"Be still my soul," I thought as I collapsed in a chair. "The Lord is on your side." The hymn, to the tune Finlandia, began to float through my mind. "Bear patiently the cross of grief or pain. Leave to your God to order and provide; in every change God faithful will remain. Be still my soul your best, your heavenly friend, through thorny ways leads to a joyful end."

I opened my hymnal for the second and third verses. "Be still my soul; your God will undertake, to guide the future as in ages past. Your hope and confidence let nothing shake; all now mysterious shall be bright at last. Be still my soul; the waves and wind still know, the Christ who ruled them while He dwelt below." I read on. "Be still my soul; the hour is hastening on, when we shall be forever with the Lord; when disappointment, grief and fear are gone, sorrow forgot, love's purest joys restored. Be still my soul; when change and tears are past, all safe and blessed we shall meet at last." This hymn had become so profound in this moment!

The diligent care continued. Every three hours Sally was turned and repositioned on one side and then the other. Pillows were placed between her knees. "Turn and kiss" became the phrase. Every time she was turned, I would kiss her for each family member, rub her with vanilla scented body lotion. A precious oil for a dear sister.

At one point, Sally looked at me with pleading eyes and garbled; "I . . . on't . . . ant . . . t . . . die."

I turned to Tanya, the night nurse saying, "Did she say what I think she said?"

She nodded, and I buried my face in Tanya's shoulder hiding my tears. Sally looked so frightened and childlike.

Hours passed and Sally was now sleeping. This hospital had its own set of TV channels. One was on Death and Dying; another on Birth and Newborns. Sally loved the one on newborns and now that she slept, I switched on the Death and Dying channel and was soon mesmerized by beautiful guitar music, and the reading of psalms and scripture. Along with a soaring eagle, I was lifted over mountains and roaring waterfalls. This must have been the bible belt! Would this program be available in New England? I was grateful, however, that Sally was hearing soothing, peaceful music, and that it was providing me with such comfort.

I was emotionally drained and lay limp in the atmosphere around me. Sally's room had become a sacred place, and I felt like a sponge drinking it in.

"Blessed are they that mourn for they shall be comforted." Comfort was everywhere and it came in abundance.

"Hello". . . a voice broke into my revelry. "My name is Reverend Linda Arnold, one of the hospital chaplains." One look at Sally and she instinctively opened her arms.

Unable to find a voice, I gratefully accepted her embrace. "Please pray with me and Sally that she comes to a peaceful acceptance of her passing."

Taking Sally's hands we formed a circle, and as Reverend Arnold prayed, I felt a peace flowing through me. A peace that had power, a power that I visualized flowing from one hand to the next and back again. "Where two or three are gathered," I thought, "there is the Lord." We formed a circle, no beginning and no end, eternity.

Midnight and the bathing, turning and rubbing of sweet smelling lotion every two hours continued. When I could, holding her hand, I would lay my head on her bed and try to rest. Every once in a while there were long pauses in Sally's breathing. "Apnea," I was told, not a good sign.

At about 2:20 am, Sally was lovingly turned again. The pillow between her knees and the tubes were all repositioned. I noticed that there was no color in her lips, her breathing was very shallow, there was a crackle to it. I sensed that this was the end. Holding her hand, I cried, kissed her forehead and she took one more final breath . . . making me jump from the unexpected gasp! I sobbed and told her how sorry I was. I looked at the clock. It was 2:29 am.

In a few moments I left the room to look for a nurse. "She's gone . . . she's gone." I cried. The night nurse was very sympathetic and told me she would call the coroner to pronounce her.

Pronounce her? Announce her? It almost sounded the same. Was she not at that moment being announced into the Kingdom of God? The kingdom where love rules . . . where love had been proven to rule. A love that had welded this family together. Love, the only all pervading reality that continued to survive and rise up out of this nightmare of a disease.

At my request, Reverend Arnold came into the room. The night nurse was repositioning Sally onto her back, pushing all the paraphernalia to the side.

"He descended into hell;" had new meaning. It was that part of The Apostles' Creed that was hard to understand. Why should Christ descend into hell before ascending into heaven? Now here it was repeated in Sally's suffering. An affirmation that "nothing can separate us from the Love of God." Had Sally not been through hell with this disease? Was she not now free of the pain and suffering of this hell?

Sally had two parents who could not have loved her more. She was brought into this world in love, and clearly had been born out of this world with Love. "God is Love." Love was all pervasive. Love had cut down all the walls that occasionally divide a family. Love was a resurrection in itself, above the hell of death. If "God is Love," then God was surely present.

The night light on the wall behind her head gave her face an ethereal look. I took her comb and combed her hair out over her pillow. I picked an orchid and placed it behind her ear. She looked like Ophelia, floating on the water.

"There," I thought, "now you are ready."

"She looked truly beautiful and truly at peace. For the next two hours and twenty minutes, I sat holding her hand and made the necessary phone call to Gerry. He would come to the hospital soon. Then I called Penelope. I asked her to go in person in the morning to tell Mom. In that darkened room with its sweet smells and beautiful music, I made those calls. I felt an overwhelming peace and privilege at Sally's passing. I was glad the coroner was late and that I had had this length of time.

Penelope said, "I wish I were there. I can't believe she is lying right beside you."

"I'll put the phone to Sally's ear for you. You talk to her; you are here as much as I am." I could only make out a few words of the sweet sister-to-sister "I love you's." There was a feeling of peace in that dimly lit hospital room.

It was 5:00 am and Gerry was taking me to the airport. He needed to make a quick stop at home where he had stayed in the Virginia country side. The moon was very full and very high, the sunrise was imminent.

"I'll be in soon Gerry . . . I need to stretch and get some air."

As I strolled around to the back of the house, I could see my breath in the cool pre-dawn air. I had been told that there were deer around the house all the time. Sure enough, I heard a rustle and a beautiful buck appeared at the edge of the woods. He had an enormous spread of antlers. He paused as if surprised to see me, then turned and bounded away.

Awesome power and peace . . . a presence that stayed with me on my tearful flight home.

It Moves

BY JAMIE LEE MEADS

I like the sparkle and the way it move.
I like my mother and the way she move.
I like the other one too, and the way she move,
when she laugh.
Yeah, I like these chilly breezy days, too,
and the way they move.
The breath, alive like dragons,
these days.
The way we move . . .
Not so predictable anymore.
Like that day she up and moved,
right quick and sad away from me.
I guess I even like the way that move.
Time and heat and heavy things.
Seas and willows and coyotes.

Wisteria pods, full, like they gonna cry.
Cryin' that never stop.
It right outside this window.
And it cry for me every day.

But them hills over there, they don't move.
I keep watchin' and waitin',
but, nothin'.
I guess that's pleasin', too.
Your face, it's never still.
Like my mind, always
headin' somewhere.
Not even sleep, and not even grief
could keep us still.

So, I like the way that move too.
(And you know what?)
My heart . . .
Well, that move for you.

Domestic Meditation

BY JEBBA M. HANDLEY

I stand serene before the shelves of my linen closet
Running my hands over the soft-hued stack of sheets,
wishing I could fold the fitted bottoms
as neatly as I do the large luxurious tops.

Ironed smooth and redolent of lavender,
the layered colors please my eye.
I realign the twin-sized cases
before touching the treasured European squares.
These lie folded in meticulous rectangles,
their scalloped flanges, their hemstitched ruffles
arranged just so.
Like a child I choose for them the favored place,
the center shelf.

I gaze at them,
Lace upon lace, pattern upon pattern, nation upon nation,
knowing patient hands around the world have fashioned these.
I do not let their makers down.
I lavish starch,
and iron and loving care upon them.

And when I make the beds I am most playful,
Interspersing Cretan cases with Portuguese geometries,
Roman damasks with Parisian stripes.

I wish our world were like this closet,
so sweetly do these nations here combine
to make a welcome bed.

Heroine

BY SUZANNE MCCONNELL

Now at last I sing of you
Because you are unsung
Mother, Mom, Mama,
Whose given name is Grace

Papa was the dark star
the thunderhead
naturally I gave him my speech:
swallowed, raged, grieved,
forgave

While you were there
like the house I lived in
like growing bones,
skin, air

In illness
now again
he is the acute
you the chronic

Your day revolves around him.
You are small; so is he.
You pull, you haul.
You lean over the regular
back-breaking bed

You with the pain
of arthritis
You with no-breath
emphysema
You who've lost ten pounds
A small old lady
precious blue eyes

Nightly, daily
you achieve heroine's feats
Pulling down his pajamas
fumbling to remove
the adult diapers
huge on his bony
stroke-struck body
tucking another diaper under
hauling the clean pajamas up
one leg, the other,
the arduous lift and stretch
over hips

Wriggling the damp tee shirt
pushing his well arm through taut sleeve
maneuvering over head
tugging, wrenching
off at last
sliding it down the floppy shrunken limb
You take the clean shirt
start again

You bring him
oatmeal in the morning
fruit processed to a sauce at noon
juice, milk, coke,
three chocolate malts
ground meat and potatoes at night
Turn television on and off
go to the john
nap inbetween.

You say "I eat well.
Worry has made me thin."

But as you bend
I hear you gasp
I see your shoulder bone
poked up, spread awry
your knuckles big with it
your joints that ache
that know
the rain comes

Papa wants you
to stay on the couch
across from him
to curl up there
while he naps
sitting up in his bed

And you do
You do it all
as you always have.

I sing of you
mother my blue-eyed love
and ask forgiveness
for all my love unsung

An Aria

BY JADENE FELINA STEVENS

Whenever I hear an operatic baritone
father, I think of you

of how you studied in Milan while mother
sent packages, cared for two babies.

I remember you when I was four.
I remember when you came to see me

twenty-five years later. You no longer sang
your heart grown too weak.

Where are all the songs you sang
and to whom?

Was a single aria ever for me?

Whenever I hear an operatic baritone
I think of you, father

of how my mother kept a black and white photograph
of you, costumed as the clown in Rigoletto.

Did you ever grace her fidelity with a song?

I know how you must have looked
as you paused, on stage, one hand

on your breast, your throat muscles
tensed and you

breathing my mother's devotion
into your lungs, giving back false notes

and a divorce
to celebrate your first performance.

. . . I cannot carry a true note.

I have lived in a world of muffled sound

imagining opera houses
murals by Michaelangelo

angels, white wings suspended in flight
as they listened to your arias, listened

to what I could not hear . . .

For Filipo "Phillip" Acciavatti

Love Moves

BY LETTIE P. COWDEN

It is the time
The time of my blood
Of sitting in
Its fertilities
Holding babies, like
Plucked and glabrous chickens
Up high, high in my arms
It is the effulgent time
Oh, it is, believe it—!
Sucking up the earth
In full efflorescence
Owning the earth
And the earth owning you
Dear God, death
Is a long, unbelieved bridge
Stretching far from where
You sit in your moisture
Or where, readied
You lie making guttural noises
And love moves
With this husband, or
With that lover.

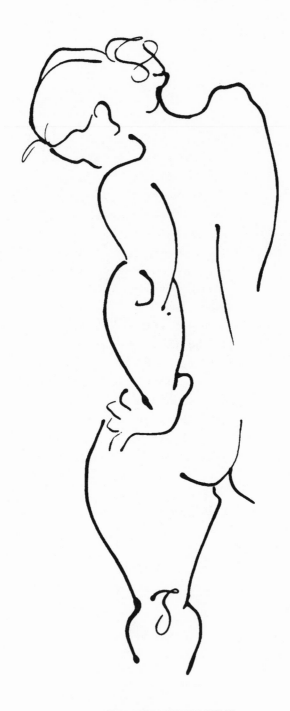

KAREN KLEIN, INK DRAWING

I V

Passages and Transformations

The Only Constant

BY ANNE D. LECLAIRE

CHANGE is the only constant.

You'd think at this point in my life, I would be accepting of this truth, yet change is overtaking me this season. The seasonal shift—so dramatic here on Cape Cod—seems this year to mirror the transformation in my own internal and external landscapes.

Bulldozers invade the vacant lots on either side of our property. To the east, a young man erects his first house. To the west, the lot is being prepared for the home we are building for my mother, a woman of fierce independence who, widowed and feeling the betrayal of an aging body, has surrendered some measure of her autonomy in order to be close to us, to live in a house she will no longer have to shoulder the burden of.

The home she and my father lived in for the past twenty-five years is sold. As we crate her belongings for the move, I operate on automatic pilot, finding refuge in organization, in packing and cleaning, in crossing off chores on a master list. Days later, emotions—which we can run from but never escape—catch up. I am troubled to be confronting my mother's aging, my own vulnerability, our mortality. Although he has been gone for ten years, I mourn my father's death. Again I do the heavy work of grief.

Nothing is static. Our across-the-street neighbor has died. He recently celebrated his ninety-ninth birthday and his was surely a full life by anyone's reckoning, yet I am saddened. For thirty-two years his benevolent gaze has blessed our home and his passing leaves the neighborhood indelibly altered, lessened.

More changes follow. Too many, too fast, too profound. My heart is confused and full with the extremes of life.

My sister's first grandchild is born. My two children talk about their upcoming college graduations. Birth and death and change perforate the fabric of our family, and I experience a rising anxiety about the impermanence and transitory nature of life. A child of western culture, I have a deep attachment to the belief that we can dominate our inner and outer environments. An illusion, I know, for to arrest change is impossible. As impossible as stopping life itself. It is surrendering to it, making peace with it that is our work.

I call a friend who is herself in an eddy of change. "How are you coping?" I ask as we talk about her new position at work, her search for a new rental, her recent bout of illness. "I'm exhausted," she confesses. The trick, she has come to believe, is to ride the wheel of change instead of railing against it.

In the midst of all this, I head for the beach, seeking solace in a walk by the ocean. There, as my feet make their temporary prints in sand, I am reminded of another, inland sea. I recall the rolling expanse of a mid-western prairie and, remembering, at last I find consolation.

For four of the past five autumns, I have lived for a month on the edge of a tall grass prairie in Illinois. Each October, I have stood witness as the grasses are set afire, whole swatches erased by flame. In the aftermath of the blaze, charred ashes of goldenrod, asters and reeds blacken the earth underfoot. The prairie, formerly an ocean of flowering grasses that swayed about my shoulders as I walked its trails, seems lost. The cloying, acrid smell of smoke clings to my clothes and coats my throat. My shoes are stained with soot. I mourn the loss of the prairie I had grown to love. The delicate blues and yellows of its flowers. The every present dance of bugs and butterflies weaving through its greens. All gone.

And yet, just days after the fire, minute shoots rise up out of the blackened remains, tender growth kindled by the nutrients of burned vegetation. New life born of and fed by the old.

Remembering the prairie, I find comfort in the memory of the fire, in the knowledge of the riches that change can effect, and in the understanding that even in the guise of devastation change is continually the bedrock for new life. Change *is* life. If, in the moment, I am unable to embrace the prospect of the "ever-whirling wheel of change," I can at least manage some frail accommodation of it.

"Let the great world spin forever down the ringing groove of change," Tennyson wrote.

The challenge, as always, is in facing this unknown groove not with the constriction of fear but with the power of faith.

FRANCIE RANDOLPH, "IN THE MOMENT OF UNRAVELING"
SOLAR PLATE INTAGLIO PRINT, 2001

Where Things End

BY MARY DOERING

I did not know time
could collapse backwards, enter rooms
drawn from memory
or how quickly I would walk through those rooms
still planning my escape
shivering in the deep shadows of familiar places

I still don't know how
to pull back the curtains, let in the light
      without going blind
how to unfocus the eye that saw too much
yet cannot seem to see where things end
or begin, where they go forward or reverse

I did not know when I held up the mirror
the first face I'd see would be my own,
or how young I was
when I began to keep score
and I did not know, that even after all these years
there would remain, this small fist of fingers
still counting

The Diagnosis

BY ANITA MEWHERTER

Words that change your life
        should be pronounced in an ancient cathedral
        where faint shafts of light
        stream through stained-glass windows
                or
        a hushed panelled courtroom
        where great leather chairs
        stand in ponderous attention
                not
        in cramped sterile cubicle
        furnished in chrome
        with a lonely chipped sink
        and one red plastic chair

And I . . . I, dressed only in paper
        with my heart in a knot
        and my feet cold and dangling

        Am frozen in time

If That Mockingbird Don't Sing

BY ROBIN L. SMITH-JOHNSON

All day I tried to make sense
of the words: baby's dead.
Instead, I pushed objects around:
dustcloth, broom, mop, broken glass.
I broke two glasses that morning.
The bright shards stuck to my fingers.

Earlier on the beach,
chair tucked close to chair,
we had sat and spun the future.
Our heads bent together,
we made one shadow.
Around us, the children played.

Then you stroked your belly,
said I feel him moving.
Like a fish swimming underneath?
You smiled, then nodded.
There was sand between our toes
and bits caught in the long strands of your hair.

In a dream, the baby is himself,
friend to my youngest child.
His blonde hair shines in the sun.
There are hands beckoning him
and he runs, laughing behind a rock.
His voice reaches me like a wave breaking.

Ashes

BY ANNE GARTON

ALL WINTER, AND WELL INTO SPRING, I collect buckets of wood ash from the floor of my fireplace. I spread them all around the garden. I shovel them into the compost bin, under the blueberry bushes. I've been doing this as long as I can remember. I do it because this is what my father taught me. I think it's the right thing to do. It's the old way.

My real name is Angela, my mother's middle name. No one ever calls me Angela. I can count on one hand the Angela's I know, which is why that book *Angela's Ashes* made such an impression on me. It was written by Frank McCourt. He won a Pulitzer for it. They made a movie. You might think it was a book about his mother, Angela, but of course, it's all about Frankie. Then I started to think about the *ashes*. Angela's ashes. It's the whole title.

Angela and I share more than a name. We share a weird attraction to ashes, maybe even a fetish. It seems to me that Angela's fixation on the ashes in her grate is something her son imagined—like a kind of madeleine bringing back his entire childhood. We don't know what *she* was thinking. She didn't write her own story. Her job was to stir those ashes long enough to put *life* back into something that seemed utterly dead; to keep on stirring until a small flame ignited whatever bits of coal her sons found on the street. It's a shame. All she'll be remembered for now is one half of a deadly epithet. Angela's Ashes. Whatever happened to poor Angela's own ashes, I thought.

But the ashes I scatter around my garden come from luxury, from fires in my living room, fires for delight—unnecessary fires. You have to love a fire if you want enough ashes, which is why I keep one going, more or less, all winter. The other day when I lugged my pail out to the garden I was thinking, is there anything more deadly than ashes? I am tossing *death* around like fertilizer—pulling life back through the half-death of winter. I spread these flyaway, nauseating, insubstantial particles over the garden and I am thinking how biblical it is. Dust to dust. Ashes to ashes. There's something about fire and ashes that bring all these contradictions to mind. I think I must be linked through this pale connection to something ancient, some secret woman-knowledge. Maybe that's what the other Angela was thinking too.

Who figured it out? What ancestral stirrer of ashes dragged that first pail out from the cave thinking maybe something good will come of it? How did she know? She'd have been timid at first. Everyone might laugh. And then, later, as the years went by, she would have thrown those ashes around with confidence. Brava! So would the others. By then they'd have figured it out. Maybe she saw how the forest springs back after a fire, and for her that's enough. Maybe there was an ashes god just for women. An ashes *goddess*. Who knows? Well, if it's in the bible it goes back a long way. Dust to dust.

I remember when I first learned about the power of ashes. My father and I would clean out the woods behind our cottage every spring, lopping off all the dead branches and cutting down the dying, rotten trees. We'd gather dead brush and limbs and all the leaves, and we'd burn them up in a huge bonfire. A gift from the forest gods, he'd say. Then, in the morning, after the sacrifice, after cooking our meal over it and warming ourselves beside it, we'd take the deadness of watered down ashes out to the woods and we'd thread them through the trees. And that's how we kept our woodlot healthy. As I said, my father taught me this. He's dead himself, now. Dust to dust.

But I might have had those childhood fires in mind one night when I spotted Aunt Milly in an antique ice bucket behind the glass doors of an old sideboard in my friend Margaret's apartment. Of course, I didn't know it was Milly at the time. I only knew that, right across from where I was sitting, in the middle of a very nice dinner party, there was a shiny silver ice bucket I'd never seen before. It was odd, that ice bucket, sitting there on the shelf, unused; no ice. Margaret and I know each other's houses intimately (we have *keys*) and this is a *new*, old ice bucket.

"Why aren't we using that gorgeous bucket?" I ask my friend, following her into the kitchen, plucking ice from an old salad bowl.

"In a minute, dear." She sweeps back into the dining room with her apricot bundt cake, aflame on its pedestal, and the party carries on. I'm back at the table, staring at the bucket.

"Maggie—you know that ice bucket?" I say at the door when we are ready to leave, everyone else gone home. She laughs and pulls me back into the dining room.

"You'll never guess . . ." she says, sliding the bucket out of the sideboard. She holds it towards me in both hands. "It's Aunt Milly!"

"Milly? I don't get it. You mean . . . her *ashes*? In an *ice bucket*?"

"Oh, I don't know," she shrugs, "it seemed right at the time." She puts Milly's ice bucket back in the sideboard.

Well, well. Millicent McDonald, Director of Intimate Apparel at Macy's Department Store in New York City, retired. And dead last year, at eighty-seven. Aunt Milly, come to rest in an antique ice bucket on a shelf in the sideboard of her only niece's Victorian dining room, right where I wouldn't miss her. Where no one would.

I could smell her perfume in the room with us; that's how vivid she was.

I thought a lot about Milly that night and the next day. A friend's ashes should have a sobering affect. Later, I drop by Margaret's apartment and, after some pointless conversation, I ask if I can see the ashes.

"You want to *look* at them? Take the lid off?"

"Well, yeah," I say, and leave it at that. I don't know why I want to, and I'm glad she doesn't ask.

She pulls the bucket out of the sideboard again. I can smell Milly's minty breath now. I can feel her bony hand in mine, the weight of her head as it rested on my shoulder in the car, driving back from somewhere. I hear that old flinty voice, cracking her worn-out jokes.

The bucket is almost half full. Milly's ashes are a little chunkier than my wood ashes. And there's a slight coloration to them. I'd say biscuit colored. I resist the urge to touch them, stick my finger in the bucket, twirl the ashes around, taste them. I have all those urges, but I resist them.

"Pretty amazing, huh?" she says. "I mean, when you think about Milly . . . ." Her voice trails off.

I don't know what to think. "Milly is just too—insubstantial like this," I say.

"Well, I *guess so*," she laughs, putting the bucket back where anyone sitting facing the kitchen can see it. "Not much to Milly these days."

I don't tell her this, but I find the whole thing really shocking. Milly is inconceivably somewhere among this pile of pale stuff, all that was Milly, all of her pretensions, her mid-Atlantic accent, her smoker's cough, her halitosis and opinions, her turned-down mouth and skinny shoulders that collapsed when you hugged her. Milly, maiden lady, the much-teased and beloved only aunt, the dinner guest who came and stayed and stayed, especially after she moved to Boston, bringing us boxes of dainty underpants wrapped in tissue and a bustier for each of our daughters from the Intimate Apparel Department of Macy's Department Store. Aunt Milly who said she never once found love.

"This can't be *all* of it?" I say, "All of Milly. There's not *enough*." I am close to tears. Margaret looks at me. I think she's annoyed. "Well, it *is*," she snaps. "Where did you think she was?"

Who would keep their favorite aunt in a sideboard, looking right out at you when you're trying to eat your dinner, I ask myself.

She puts the bucket back into the sideboard, smiling,

"Milly always loved a good party," she says.

Well, yes she did, I think.

I am spreading my woody ashes the next day, but I am thinking of Milly in the ersatz urn. A Milly spent is a Milly urned. I laugh. She would have liked that. A bad little joke.

But it is a cool November afternoon and my mind soon wanders over to death again, as if it were taking itself on a little walk through rotting leaves. I think about Milly in the ice bucket and my fireplace ashes. The great dead-end. Death in a dying month, death everywhere. And I imagine Milly sifting through my fingers. This is the darkening month I gave birth to my first child. Birth. Death. And in my mind that afternoon and the following morning, Milly's ashes and those faraway days of forest clearings with my much-missed father and my own fireplace gleanings spread through the garden and my daughter's birth all come together and I have one of those moments when I think life is comprehensible after all.

The next day I take my key to Margaret's house and, while we both should be at work, I visit Milly in the ice bucket. I take it out of the sideboard and this time I don't resist. I stir the ashes with my finger. And I taste them. I smudge them on my chin and on my forehead. And then I do something unthinkable, maybe criminal. I add a bag full of my own fireplace ash to Milly's and stir it all together. I fill the urn to the top.

The texture is different now, but already she seems bigger, more important, the way she was in life. I like it. I like the whole idea. Now I am adding the woods and my fireplace and November fires and memories of my father and those long-ago forest purges and childbirth into whatever is left of Margaret's most unforgettable relative. I think of that Irish Angela, that desperate mother whose story we'll never know but whose ashes are immortalized, and I'm adding her too. I'm making more of Milly. Of Angela. I'm giving them serious volume, which they deserves.

I hesitate. Maybe too much. I take a handful of the mixed ash and put it in with what's left of my own ashes. I've missed you Milly, I say. I loved you. I'm taking you home to my garden.

AMY SZEP, PENCIL DRAWING

High Tide

BY JAMIA KELLY

golden satin glass
salt spun
gently rocking
in deceptive union
float surrendered
drifting weightless
on a million salt tears
disguised as silk
shot with light
feathered sailboats
rock in rhythm on the tide,
floating
sweet surrender.

My grandfather's ghost
rests beside me on the sand,
and his gifts to me
are water,
and the smell of seaweed in the sun,
and a dream of skimming
over waves to find new anchorage
somewhere beyond
the silver far horizon.

Thirty

BY KRISTIN KNOWLES

My first gray hair
sprung forth directly above
the center of my forehead,
as I imagine Athena must have
sprung from the head of Zeus,
and it boldly stood straight up,
crooked as my pinkie finger
and wiry as silver thread.
I showed it off to all my friends
and swore I'd never dye,
deny, or disguise it,
this trophy of my years,
twisting upward like the fingers
of each branch of a winter locust
summoning the change of the seasons.

As my thirtieth birthday approached,
in an unforeseen fit of adolescent defiance,
I plucked that willful weed,
callously casting it aside
while I preened my golden youth.
Later, ashamed of my impulsive act,
I put it in a little glass charm box
with rose petals, quartz crystals,
the stolen locks of a lost lover's curls . . .
all sacred treasures and keepsakes
of something I feared would be forgotten,
lost forever in the maze of my memories
unless I held on to some tangible trinket.

I realize now that my fear was unfounded,
for as we all know about the nature of weeds:
if you don't pull out the roots
you might as well have sown the seeds.
For these fierce little fighters
consistently come back in force,
refusing to surrender so easily.

Now I am greeted each morning
by the offspring of my original . . .
soft spoken, less brazen
but dependably there each day.
And I welcome their continual arrival,
loving their delicate distinction
and reminding myself that
weeds are just as worthy of life
as any other living thing,
and they are only "weeds,"
undesirable and condemned to die,
because we define them to be so.

Euphoria in Retirement

BY MARGUERITE AHLBERG

From my journal, February 16, 1987,
President's Day.
Our first winter on the Cape

We turned out all the lights
   sat in the dark
   and watched the moon rise
   at the bay window.

It was windy and the flagpole
   made from a broken mast
   swung back and forth
   like a metronome.

The rows of utility wires
   jumped up and down
While the moon rose through them
   quite rapidly as we watched.

And then it climbed above

   a whole note
   that had broken free
   from the bass clef staff.

Wishes...

BY THELMA TURNER

THE REALTOR CALLS. WOULD I LIKE TO look at condos? Apartments? A small cottage, perhaps. She also has listings out of state.

Not sure I want to look at anything, I say no to condos, mumble something about land. In another state. Some red rock desert land.

My eyes wander to an arrangement of colored stones struggling to blossom on the generations' old oak table at which I sit; my fingers, busy with retirement, pick at the dust stuck to their sharp alien surfaces. Red and tan, pale purple and green, small pieces from the mountains in New Mexico.

"What time can we meet?" she asks.

"I need to check a few things. Let me call you back."

I wish I could move on—past this line I carve in the sand. On this insulated isthmus. Adrift in amniotic fluid.

Messages babble over the answering machine, come in the mail. Add to the pile already on the table. Some opened, most not. An order form for plants and bulbs pokes out the bottom. It was due last fall. A spring one came today.

Outside the sun shines. Shadows form. Rain moves in. A surrogate night displaces day.

In the garden, there are no new tulips, daffodils, narcissus. Only gaps where a yellow, a white, a red should have been. And the rose bushes that were to decorate the new fence separating a no man's land of cat briar and pitch pine from the lawn are but limp fantasies in my mind.

"I don't know what happened," I tell my friend. "Every spring I plant perennials, roses. Every fall I order bulbs. Holing them into the ground renews a faith that spring will come. I didn't buy any last year. Here's the order—filled out, but no check, no envelope, no stamp, and so, of course, no mailing, no replacements, no new plants."

"Oh, well, there's always next year," my friend says.

"Even the year before when I ordered bulbs, I planted them so late most of them turned to mold or dust before I got them in the ground. A few came up—scrawny with pale leaves, no flowers."

"You'll have to get at your ordering—and planting—earlier next year."

I agree.

Outside I rake last fall's leaves, burn this spring's broken twigs, winter's fallen limbs. Throw away old seeds, look in stores for new ones, just a few, to recapture a sporadic enthusiasm that pops up every December, with holiday shopping, tree trimming, parties done up in cheery red and green. Which, this January, took a nosedive—to the lowest level. Where it got stuck. An apparition of the past.

Then there's the microwave, the big, over five-hundred-dollar convection-conversion job that I couldn't lift, that stayed in its box for months after my move to Cape Cod, waiting for a visit from my son in New York to haul it out, put it on the counter. The microwave that was to last the rest of my whole new life. No cooking, no stove for me. Just nuke it, eggs, oatmeal, anything.

"What's that noise?" this same son asks. He's visiting for the weekend.

"Microwave. The fan. It struggles, stops, starts up again."

"It must take a long time to heat stuff. Your electric'll go up."

I call the appliance repairman.

"Problem is," I tell him, "the fan. It comes on slow. Works—intermittently."

"Can you bring it into the shop?"

"Too heavy. I can't lift it."

"I won't be able to get there until sometime next week."

But the microwave doesn't wait till next week. A couple of days later it pops a spark. I shut the thing off. Unplug it. Call the repairman again to let him know the latest.

"A service call alone is thirty-five dollars," he informs me.

"Do you have any idea how bad the problem is? Is it worth fixing?"

"Ten years old, you say? Well, from what you've told me, the fan and motor are probably both shot. And if that's the case, it'll cost well over two hundred dollars to get it working again."

"Let me think about it."

I wish it hadn't blown. I wish I didn't have to decide its fate. Fix it because it looks good on its special shelf, a good back up for my apartment-size stove—or pick up a new one on sale? Certainly no more than a hundred for a new one.

A child moves west. Another east. A third into my heart, rebelling all the way. The fourth still torn in two. He says, inside his mind, he's still trying to reconcile his father and me—where, without meaning to, we must still be doing battle.

"I hate the holidays," he told me last Christmas, "when I have to choose."

The marriage broken—
The lovers gone—
Far from old friends—
—moved to this beach land—where, summers and summers ago, the children and I used to vacation. Moved to this too big house—which was to have been a place for them to come. But it's different now, not the same as when we had to plan and save and travel the better part of a day to get here. And even though they visit and especially after they visit, I keep an empty house.

Four a.m. awakens me with seeming trivialities, band-aids for the pain.
Long ago I buried pain.

I wish my grandmother had had more than a crust of bread to eat for too, too many days. I wish she hadn't had to mother brothers and sisters. I wish she hadn't hidden in the cellar when thunderstorms battered and bruised the sky.

I wish my mother hadn't screamed at the whir and stir of bees, wasps and hornets and all things that buzz the air. I wish she'd known how capable and intelligent and talented she was. I wish she hadn't cleaned my grandmother's house, top to bottom, twice a year, each time saying, "Try to keep it this way," after she'd finished.

I wish my father hadn't had to stand behind the plow behind the horse—he too short to see over the handles of the plow, the horse's back—when he was only ten. I wish his mother and father hadn't taken him out of school to plant and harvest crops. I wish he could have finished eighth grade.

I wish he'd bought one of the many farms he looked at when I was young. Not settled for a white bungalow in a small town on the U-shaped street where I grew up.

I pour a cup of coffee, place it in the microwave, push the right buttons. But I forget, it's broken. A black cave inside. Then I remember.

I haven't called the repairman back.

I haven't made up my mind.

I call.

"Is it worth fixing?" I ask again.

He must not remember I called before or does remember and has nothing new to add and so with extra kindness says, "I'll talk to Joe. He's the real expert on these old dinosaurs."

Dinosaurs, I think, who needs dinosaurs?

But I'm polite.

"I'd appreciate that," I say.

"Call you back. Let you know."

But I don't need him to call me back. I already know.

I scoop up piles of papers strewn about, stuff them into manila envelopes, rearrange the centerpiece of variegated rocks on the old oak table over which I bend;

pour leftover coffee in a pan, put it on the stove to heat;

look outside where the fence I planned to smother in rambling red roses casts unencumbered shadows. The shadows—except for a solitary one that walks beside me—are behind me now.

Pale Skin Breathing

BY MARY DOERING

a young girl her feet bare
stands at the edge of the ocean
she has no map
no knowledge of stars
no deep primordial memory
to lead her back to fresh water

all she hears are waves
washing up, dragging pebbles
back over rocks

yet underneath always
another sound
thick, complicated
like desire or disappointment
pulling itself into her body

a bone deep tide
disturbing all things
not yet come to the surface

in the dark they wait
their closed eyelids a delicate purple
and each vertebra
clearly visible
through pale skin breathing

Selling the House

BY JUNE BEISCH

Every day, the soft murmur of
strange voices moving through my rooms
disturbing the universe. The baskets of
dried grass on the rafters, star quilts asleep
on the upstairs beds. Invasion of privacy!

The hanging spider plant clings to my shoulder
as I pass. Strange footsteps on my cellar stairs.
A salutary storm of sobs as some young child
complains and weeps about moving again.

The blond realtor pirouettes into the room.
She will tell the strangers that this is an old house,
a house that has been loved, that we would
certainly stay but for the sound of our own
voices, but for the way the days slide away fast,
we might linger, finishing up the dishwashing
after the important dinner.

And I would stay if I were not
a woman with a For Sale sign for a heart,
a woman looking to spend her remaining years
grander, in a house with more chandeliers.

Be Careful With My Dead Body...

when you shoot
it down the chute
to the basement
of some funeral parlor
where corpses hold court like
lords and ladies in the Middle Ages did.
True, bones and flesh
can now be fixed with no pain to me;
nevertheless, one request:
Keep my body right side up,
don't drop it on its head.

Don't poison it
with chemicals,
drain its blood,
suck out visceral organs.
Don't throw any of them away.

Don't paint its cheeks
with blush, its lips gloss-pink,
dress it up in blue chiffon,
white lace upon the trim.
Don't fold one hand upon the other
so diamonds and rubies
can glitter in perfect repose.

It is no party
to which it goes;
there is no noble end
to where it's been,
no grim demise—so
dry your eyes,
stifle your cries.

Lay it out
not in a mahogany bed,
with satin puckered and pleated
about its head.
Lower it not
in a concrete box—
taking a millennium or more

for concrete to crumble,
the body to return to dust.

Nor would I have you take me
(when it's too late to save me)
to where lab technicians dressed
in unnatural green
remove eyes, ears
hearts, livers
and other unmentionable things.
And, oh, doctors dear,
do leave my tonsils and adenoids alone.
I've kept them through
thick and thin
of medical *mal*-practice
and would not
that death should do them in.

What *would*
I have
you do
with me?

Quite simple.
Stake my dear, sweet "bod"
on the branch of some limber tree
or down upon the ground.
Leave it for birds to eat
coyotes to mock
wolves to mourn
jackals and hyenas to gnaw upon,
a speck here and there
for insects to discover.

Oh, do be careful with my dead body.
In its cold chrysalis
lies the DNA of all the lives
I have yet to live,
an energy
I am endless part
and sacred parcel with.

— BY THELMA TURNER

Black Stockings

BY GERRY DI GESU

Age 5-12. St. Michael's Elementary School. Sister David roughly pulls back my shoulders. "Sit up straight like a lady. You never listen." Ugly, heavy, patched black stockings cover her legs. What do they wear underneath? —A good Catholic girl.

Age 13-18. St. Mary's High School. "Get that smirk off your face. Try and act like a lady for a change. I don't see much hope for you anyway." Black cotton stockings droop around Sister Agnes' fat ankles. Do they ever think about sex? Each night in bed I hide beneath the covers, flashlight in hand praying penitential prayers listed in my "Catholic Girls Guide." I seek forgiveness for I know I am dammed to hell if I die the next day because of perceived impure thoughts and behaviors. —A good Catholic girl.

Age 20-30. New bride. Rhythm method of birth control. "We can't. It's not the right time. Don't come near me." Blouses still button to the top and slacks and skirts fit loosely. —A good Catholic girl.

Age 30-50. Wife, mother, daughter. Three children, full time job, sick parents. "I'm tired. Try taking care of everything around here and working all day and you'd be tired too. I'm going to sleep." Business suits, gray stockings. —A good Catholic girl.

Age 50-60. Night sweats, mood swings, sagging breasts, stomach and eyelids. One big lump. "I'm sorry I hurt your feelings but I can't wear this sexy teddy. I feel like a cow."—A good Catholic girl.

Age 60+. Retired, refreshed, renewed. "Hey honey. I'm wearing black silky stockings, spike heels, lipstick, earrings and Obsession. I'm ready." —A good Catholic girl

The Encircling Gift

BY JADENE FELINA STEVENS

ON THE WAY HOME FROM GRADE SCHOOL, I'd visit certain old women who lived in my part of the Back Bay. Their friendship made me feel special, and I enjoyed hearing stories about the places they had been, and the things they had done. Visiting them was also a diversion from our cramped, one-large-room that was called a "studio apartment," and which I shared with my mother, grandmother, and younger brother. I felt almost regal as I sat with one of those old ladies in her nicely appointed brownstone home. Even though this was during the '50s, they either had Victorian furnishings, or something not far removed. I felt as though I had entered a more elegant world.

I had a *"visiting route,"* as I called it. On Monday, Wednesday, and Friday, I'd visit Mrs. Bigelow and her fat bassett hound named "Mr. Tibbs." Mr. Tibbs was too old, too arthritic, to walk very far on a leash. I'd help Mrs. Bigelow push him down Beacon Street in his worn-blue, wooden pushcart. When Mrs. Bigelow felt that we had found an appropriate spot, I'd help Mr. Tibbs out and he'd do what dogs do as he attended the sidewalk tree. Then I'd help him back in the cart and we'd continue on. After our walk, Mrs. Bigelow would serve cookies and milk from white china set on a mahogany table in her living room. I always marveled at how the afternoon light danced on the high finish of the wood, so polished, so unlike anything we had at home.

On Tuesday and Thursday, I'd visit Mrs. Gage who lived around the corner on Gloucester Street. She would hand me a slice of stale bread with instructions to break it into very small crumbs, so that the birds would not have difficulty in swallowing them. And, it went further that way, she said. She liked the small sparrows and always complained of how the larger pigeons grabbed so much, and of how the sparrows had to struggle to catch even a *"morsel,"* as she called it. There was a young maple tree planted at the edge of the brick sidewalk at her front door, and the birds would congregate there in early morning, and late afternoon, waiting for Mrs. Gage to appear.

She would invite me into her parlor with its red Persian rug floating on the floor beneath us. I imagined it was like Aladdin's magic carpet as I sipped weak coffee heavily laden with real cream, and nibbled pastries from S. S. Pierce. She liked to tell stories about her childhood home on the coast of Nova Scotia, and of the shipwrecked men like her father, who never returned.

Most days, before my other visits, an old woman dressed in a high-collared black dress would call to me, and I'd stop to chat with her for a few minutes, I standing on the steps outside her bay window, she sitting inside, in her rocking chair. I have an image of the room behind her always in shadows but that may only be because I have no clear picture of her furnishings. In all the days I talked with her, I always stood on the steps, and she always sat in her chair in the window.

I remember one particular day, my birthday, in August, when she called to me and gave me a small, beribboned box through the open window. *"For me?"* I asked excitedly, not quite sure that this unexpected gift could really be meant for me. At home, we never had very elaborate presents for any occasion, and none wrapped so elegantly as this box with its shimmering, gold-flecked paper. *"Yes, now open it, dear,"* she said, pointing to it. Slowly, I untied the bow and the golden ribbons fell away and on the white cotton I saw a bracelet with 14k gold links, freshwater pearls, and flat golden charms of sunbursts, crescent moons, and stars. I don't remember ever receiving a more royal, or thoughtful, gift.

I wonder now if I thanked her profusely enough as I held it to the light, gold shimmering in the late afternoon sun. We usually did not have the luxury of proper stationery in the house and I may not have even sent her a thank you note.

"Here," she said, *"allow me,"* and I held my arm through the window while she clasped the bracelet around my wrist.

That night, Mother told me not to wear it to school because it was too good. Later, when I went to my shoebox of special things to retrieve it, it was gone. And, years later, I found the pawn ticket in my mother's old trunk.

Now, this nameless old woman's face is only a blur. All I can remember is a lacy black dress with a pink cameo at the throat, gray hair in a high, wide bun, and her gnarled yet delicate hands reaching through the window. Perhaps her gift, the lingering dream of it, is why, even now, heading toward my own old age, I find the images of sun, moon, and stars repeat themselves throughout my poems, my prose, and are of deep significance in my life. And perhaps I'm drawn to stargazing as a way of remembering that old woman, who touched me, who cared.

"Old woman," I find myself murmuring, as I gaze at those star-filled heavens, *"thank you."*

The Tree

BY CELIA BROWN

Golden as a marquee playing
two miles off,
it caught the light at all angles
and hung down in chains.
In fact, the leguminous
yellow at the bottom
of the driveway that belongs
to other days, and faraway.

And that's gone now, anyhow.

Except for the ghost
of a laburnum weeping,
a vision with May in it,
really, that, whenever I spy,
I want to own,
the way I wanted, back then,
to enter my life
in puffed sleeves and ringlets.

JOYCE JOHNSON, INK DRAWING

Introduction

BY CYNTHIA HUNTINGTON

I am the women often found alone
—or not found. If you think of me,
in your mind's eye, see no one standing near.
See me filling the space where I move
easily, as an animal does,
moving among the hills and trees.
Part of things, but mistaken for none.

Strong legs, strong lungs, deep sleep
alone at night in a single bunk.
Mornings, I take off my jacket in the sun,
dig my toes in cool sand. Giving way
underfoot, the earth answers back: *I am.*

There is a world apart from what we call
"the world"—where we are alive in our bodies
—I am not talking about beauty, or sex,
or anything you can see with your eyes,
but a place in which we become again
the original animal we were born to be.

I want to grow old here, wiry and brown,
with the wind in my throat.
Then disappear into all of it, vanish like dusk
into the body of air, eye of the moon snail,
wholly taken up
into the sky's imagination of light.

Senior Walks at Low Tide on the Brewster Flats

BY MARGUERITE AHLBERG

We walk in a soft warm gentle breeze
As if the weather were apologizing
   for the gloomy days just behind—
   those raw bone-chilling cold and gray
   that we think will never end.

Deer tracks deep in the soft sand
   and a trim of little beads of pebbles
   left along the high tide line
   where receding waves deposited them
Leaving their artwork behind.

We pass two horseshoe crabs
   the big female with the male
   mounting from behind.
Pick up both tails together
   carry them to the incoming tide
   and watch as they become immersed.

In the haze we hear ducks gurgling
   and in a few moments we can
   just make out the flock of them
Flying low over the water.

At the eelgrass I write my prayers
   with a shell in the sand.

Twilight

BY J. LORRAINE BROWN

I stood on the sidewalk on the hard-packed snow and waited for my life to begin.
It was twilight and everything was blue.
I saw the bus, yellow, move over the top of the hill.
It rolled to a stop in front of me and I waited for the doors to open.

It was twilight and everything was blue.
I wanted to run and meet it halfway.
It rolled to a stop in front of me, and I waited for the doors to open.
I forced myself to stand still.

I wanted to run and meet it halfway.
It was so hard to breathe without you.
I forced myself to stand still.
Your uniform was blue and I reached for your hand.

It was so hard to breathe without you.
I saw the bus, yellow, move over the top of the hill.
Your uniform was blue and I reached for your hand.
I stood on the sidewalk on the hard-packed snow and waited for my life to begin.

The Rock

BY TESSA RUDD

I am like a rock,
Being broken apart with every
wave, moving only when the water does,
being stepped on by feet that only complain of their pain.
I sit with the sun beating down on me.
By day I am scorching, by night I am frozen.
I, as a child, used to pick up rocks and take them
home, calling them my pets, thinking they would grow bigger.
Now I have grown.
And I have learned how much we are alike.

BARBARA COHEN, "BOATS," PENCIL DRAWING

DIANE JOHNSON, "BENCH SITTERS IN CHATHAM," WHITE-LINE WOODCUT, 1995

V

Secrets & Silences

Lipstuck, or why I became a writer

BY SUSAN POPE

"What is our first suffering? It lies in the fact that
we hesitated to speak. It was born in the moment when we
accumulated silent things within us." —Gaston Bachelard

WHEN I WAS IN SECOND GRADE I was invited to my friend Sydney's birthday party. After eating cake and ice cream at the dining room table, Sydney opened her presents. The guests had presents too: paper baskets of peanuts and candy kisses, cone-shaped party hats, whistles that unraveled into long paper tails when we blew through them, and candy lipsticks.

The lipstick looked real and I was thrilled for I had watched with fascination as my mother applied Coty's red each morning. The other girls puckered their mouths and tried their lipsticks right away, but I saved mine to enjoy later in the privacy of my bedroom. When we finished eating, I left my nut basket and lipstick by my plate where they'd be safe until I went home.

In the sunroom, we sat on the floor in a circle to play "Gossip." Sydney went first. For a moment, she pondered, then whispered a secret to Jane on her right. Jane whispered the secret to the girl on her right and thus the gossip circled the room. "Hog putty saves the day," said the last girl to receive the message. "No," Sydney said, laughing, for in the passing the words had changed. "I said 'Our dog Betty had puppies and we gave them away.'" Everyone laughed now, a laughter I delighted in.

Over and over again we went around the circle and at last it was my turn to speak the whispered message out loud. How exhilarating speaking out felt. How wonderful to evoke laughter in others, to be the center of attention for a few moments. As a child, I rarely spoke in groups. I thought of myself as, and was often told I was, shy. Now, I consider that there are times I am shy and times I am not shy.

The game continued. I was excited by the fun we were having and when my neighbor whispered the next message to me, instead of whispering it to the girl on my right as I should have done, I again said it out loud.

"You're out of turn," Sydney said. "You have to sit out the next round," She did not allow me to explain that I had not done it on purpose, that my speaking out had been an error of enthusiasm. In front of everyone, I felt humiliated and shamed. Forced to sit silent through the fun.

I did not sit, but started for home. Then I remembered the lipstick and my lust for it led me into the dining room. The table was bare; Sydney's mother had wiped it clean. In the kitchen, I asked the grownups where my lipstick was, but no one knew. For days, I begged my mother to buy me another, but she claimed she didn't know where to find one.

Who invented lipstick, anyway? Probably a man, the better to emphasize the sensuality of women's mouths. Mouths that for many decades remained predominantly closed concerning opinions, likes and dislikes, philosophies, ideas, and challenges. Beneath ruby red lips stories waited to be told, censored for the sake of not rocking the boat. Lips stuck shut with pink, red, orange and purple goo.

In high school, I glazed my lips pink or the Halloween white popular in the early sixties, but I didn't like putting on makeup every day. "Wear lipstick once," my mother said, "and you have to wear it all the time or you'll look pale." Truth be told, some days I'd remember to wear it, but often I'd forget. When I went away to college I discarded the stuff--no one in Ohio had seen my pink lips--I wouldn't look pale to them. Except for college theater productions, where makeup was part of the costume for male and female alike, I've rarely worn makeup since.

As for the unfairness of being silenced for an innocent mistake--I hadn't thought of it as censorship until recently. The subtle ways we censor each other is a current fascination of mine, something I'm paying attention to.

Thanksgiving in New Hampshire, several years ago. Seated at the table are my mother and father, my brother and his wife and myself, visiting from Massachusetts. "Next year," I said, "let's go to Fort Number Four for Thanksgiving." Fort Number Four, a nearby historical museum, held a sit down Thanksgiving dinner every year, complete with Pilgrim costumes. That morning I had watched a television program about it and it looked like fun. I was about to tell everyone how I'd always wanted to attend the Plimouth Plantation dinner, but had never gone as reservations had to be made a year ahead. The Fort dinner seemed workable. But as soon as I spoke those opening words my mother became angry.

"I have told you I never want to go out for Thanksgiving or Christmas dinner," she said. Her voice was harsh, as if she spoke to a three-year-old who had just committed a horrible act.

"I don't deserve to be spoken to in that tone," I said.

"I have told you and told you about this. I expect you to remember." There's no point in relaying more of the conversation. It is not the specifics that matter. I felt hurt and overwhelmed, not so much by the words as by the tone of voice. Friends later pointed out that my mother might have thought I was being critical of the meal she had spent hours preparing. If so there was a communications botch up for sure.

Nevertheless, I was effectively silenced and, as at Sydney's birthday party, I wanted to stand up and leave, though I did not. Considering that emotional turmoil reduces my appetite, I ate as much as I could and murmured quiet comments on the apparently acceptable topics of the birds at the feeder and the weather.

Later reflection on this interaction provided me with a possible clue to my tendency to remain silent in groups. If my mother over-reacted to so innocent a conversational topic as dinner out at Fort Number Four, then perhaps when I was a child she may have over-reacted to other minor things. Innocent let's-do-thises, suggestions coming from others, me for instance, rather than from herself or even just the enthusiastic babbling that children partake in when they are excited about something.

As a child, perhaps I made a decision, though I can't remember it, that if my words upset others the best thing to do was to remain silent. Perhaps I labeled myself as weird, since things I thought were good ideas, others apparently found dreadful. Even today, I am reluctant to invite friends to go to movies, to a concert, for a walk. Usually, I wait to be invited. My current hesitation to speak seems connected to these and other silencings experienced throughout my life. Safety means keep your mouth glued shut about personal matters. Glued shut with or without lipstick. And who is the loser when the things I care about, think about, wonder about are kept within? When those silent things accumulate, when my hesitation means others can never really come to know me?

With these stories I do not mean to blame, or to excuse or explain my recalcitrance. Now I am an adult and not held by decisions or conditionings arising from youthful interpretations of the world. For years, I have followed my innate urge to express myself, despite any hidden decision to remain silent.

As a child, I drew, painted, danced and wrote stories in a green, spiral-bound notebook. I desperately wanted to be an artist and my parents supplied me with paints and canvases and tried to set me up with lessons from the Famous Artists School. I remember the Famous Artists man coming to the house, showing me sample lessons, telling me that if I signed up I'd get a free watercolor set.

Later in my life, my parents supported my decision to return to graduate school for an M.F.A. in Writing. They visited me in Vermont when I attended a writer's conference. And of my two parents, it was my mother who seemed the most thrilled when I published a novel, buying copies, sending them to relatives.

The message seemed to be it was okay to engage in creative activities as long as I didn't talk out loud. Painting is silent, wordless. And though one uses words to write, words too are silent on the page. Private. Is this why I became a writer? So that I might speak out from the security of my study, hide behind the anonymity of the page?

"There is a direct pipeline from my heart to my mouth," a writer friend of mine recently said. Although she experienced suppression of her creative instincts as a child, she now speaks aloud with a certain ease, bringing joy and tears to others.

As for me, there is a clog in my pipeline. The heart words go to my brain, images to my eyes, but then, there is a pause. And in that pause, the guillotine blade comes down. Off with her tongue.

"What's your point?" one of my college roommates used to ask me, as if having a point was the only excuse to speak. It is true I rarely make points, more circles. Perhaps melding the lipstick and the censorship stories together is silly, my inner censor whispers. The connection tenuous and fanciful. Do the two themes circle together, do they get any-where? My intent was to reveal the circles of my mind. If my words or images click, that's okay. If not, that's okay too.

On the page I can speak fully, use the words I choose, approach an idea slowly or quickly, make points or not make points. Probe and ponder or shoot a metaphorical arrow directly into the bull's-eye. Limited only by my imagination, my vocabulary, the range of my perceptions, I can play freely, I can speak out for myself and speak out for others. And this is marvelous.

But I long for more. Is not one of the most glorious freedoms of this country the freedom to speak? I long to speak aloud, long for my words to zap through the air towards another, long for those silences within to be made vital with sound, long to bare my heart spontaneously in the moment, my voice resonant, my lips unstuck.

And I can only hope that this longing itself, so strong within me, leads me down paths where I feel free to sing. And is it grandiose of me to hope that perhaps something I write or paint might help another to free their heart's pipeline? I don't know the answers. But meanwhile, I sharpen my pencils (yes, pencils!), break out the cadmium yellow and cerulean blue, settle into my imagination and hum.

JOYCE JOHNSON, "TRURO CHURCH," WOODCUT

Secrets

BY JAMIA KELLY

fish world, deep.
finned ones keep
their own counsel,
refuse to speak
and die by the millions
as food for their gods.

ROSE BASILE, OIL ON CANVAS: "IS IT FRESH?"

I used to write

BY JUDITH PARTELOW

I used to write
when the lump in my throat
hurt so much
it splattered ink
all over paper.

I haven't written for a long time,
but suddenly life seems summed up
and my throat aches;
it aches.

I am one of the women you haven't read about before.
We never speak our insides out.
(We have too much to lose, or think we do.)
But you'll be reading all the stories anyhow
in one newspaper or another
over coffee.

For the silent women are clamoring to be heard
though you've never seen a single, printed word.

A Painter's Muse

KARRI ANN ALLRICH

IN MY REAL LIFE I AM A PAINTER, always watchful, scanning the landscape for a twist in the road or the softened edge of a tree line meeting the summer sky, the push and play of light on moving clouds. Artists in movies talk about color, spatial relationships, and abstract composition, but at real life gatherings they jockey for political position—who studied with whom, what shop makes the best frames, what gallery sells the most work. Commissions and percentages. It is here where I begin to drift. I lose my focus and only half listen. I swim with the moon in my mind's eye, silent. Immersed in watery depths I search for her with longing like a lover's hunger. The moon is my Muse. Inspiration, pure and basic. Nothing else comes close. It's that simple.

Where others are moved by concept, the pursuit of beauty, coin or status, I am moved only by her. She is the centerpiece of my practice. I could paint her every day for the rest of my life. I try sometimes to leave her out. I place my intention square in the landscape. I lose myself in distant dunes and heathered foregrounds. I push paint around the supple give of Belgian linen and fool myself that I am satisfied. The earth has its pull, too, and I give in to the pleasure of her textures and form, the riot of information that competes for my artist's attention. I choose unspoiled ground and off-road places, but it's getting harder and harder to find a piece of earth not manipulated by man. Our evidence is everywhere, insistent. Post modern. Not everyone is saddened by this.

I do love the land, this fragile strip in the sea, and as I stand drinking in the spirit of place, it grows in urgency. The painter in me struggles with intellectual concerns: edges, atmosphere and distance. Decisions are made to redraw a tree, widen the water, sharpen a curve in the salt marsh. Stepping back from the canvas I evaluate my efforts. Have I captured the time of day? The cool morning shadows or warm blush of twilight? Does the sense of place shimmer through? Is this visual prayer of mine complete? I seldom know. I only guess. There is a moment when the effort seems to wane on its own, apart from me—the artist, standing there with stained hands and an aching pelvis. The painting is done. The prayer is over . . . maybe.

The palette gets scraped, and brushes are cleaned—the painter's ritual. The message to the intellect is sent: This painting is finished. I glance at the canvas out of the corner of my eye, turn and face it, step back. A familiar nagging begins to gather in my stomach. A sigh collects deep down. Something's missing. I feel it. I ignore this implication and move on.

Later in the kitchen I start a pot of soup, chopping garlic and Vidalia onions, setting the burner on low-medium to heat the virgin olive oil. I find the big can of Italian tomatoes in the cupboard. It needs a moon. When the onions have softened I add the tomatoes and stir. Do I paint yet another moon? I stand at the sink and wash vegetables in every color. *Mis en place* is a lovely concept in efficiency. I am not an efficient cook. I toss

KARRI ANN ALLRICH, "BLESSING MOONRISE," OIL ON LINEN

and chop as I go, and hardly ever measure an ingredient. Cooking for me is like painting. And I'm a messy intuitive painter. The vegetables go into the pot, followed by a quart of broth, a handful of herbs, and pinch of sea salt. I cover the pot and turn toward the door down the hallway. The painting is calling to me.

I surrender, as always, and take my time in contemplation. The soup won't need my attention for a good while. I sit and stare at the wet canvas resting on the milk crate. The mood is strong, the dark tone conveys the shape of the land nicely. But something's missing. I seldom debate for very long. I stand and mix the familiar creamy blend of paint that reflects the illusion of moonlight and turn toward the painting that is back on my easel. I wait, expectant. This mysterious process of painting is all about expectancy. Each blank canvas that we face is like the dark new moon. The painting is already there, waiting to be brought into the light of consciousness. All possibility awaits the slow turning of creativity, the unfolding truth.

Facing an almost finished painting with the intention of adding a moon is a delicious moment. I never know beforehand what phase the moon will be. The spirit of the painting will tell me. Persephone's crescent, clear and pure . . . or the voluptuous magnetism of the full moon? My late autumn paintings cried out for the Crone's moon, that delicate fingernail hanging in the west. Today I paint a pale waxing crescent. It completes my intention, my prayer, my offering. My Muse must be honored, after all. I cannot deny her.

You might say that in my real life I am a painter. But this is not my real life. I am a lover of the moon and all her mystery. She permeates everything I do. And I give thanks to her lessons of surrender every night.

Amaryllis

BY JUNE BEISCH

You will bloom,
in spite of all malfeasance, all
screened-in rooms. Out here on the porch,
your red petals bugle out as if to say
you will bloom
in spite of this rain-filled day, this gloom.
The birds having already quit the feeder,
having lost their taste for sunflower seeds,
the lawn having already turned to yellow
and it's only June.
Coming upon you, I find your bright flowers
balancing on that thick green stem with all
the insouciance of young girls
who insist upon mattering.

Emily Dickinson had that insouciance, too,
and she, too, insisted upon mattering,
although one critic called her "that little
home-keeping person;" although she, too,
was "late flowering"

and hid herself
for such a long, long time.

I Come From . . .

BY JEBBA M. HANDLEY

I come from the land of whispers, sit up straight, eat what's on your plate,
say thank you.

I come from the land of whispers, a best friend by my side in the dark.

I come from the land of whispers, a voice saying you're no good, give it up,
relinquish the task.

I come from the land of whispers, my Mother's voice saying try, you can do it,
saying if you fall, get up and try again.

I come from the land of whispers, a lover's whispers, laughing whispers, connu-
bial whispers.

I come from the land of whispers, my daughters' night-time secrets, my promises
to them.

I come from the land of whispers, God's voice saying, cherish the friend,
the day, the storm. Life is short.

Eyedance

BY BETH SEISER

ON THE FIRST NIGHT OF THE FIRST DAY that the new phone book came out with Sig's ad in the yellow pages, he got a call. He dozed stretched out on the couch, the TV glowing, the ringing phone pulling him from his dreams. He elbowed up on the knotty green material and headed down the hall. A cockroach skittered into the molding when he flipped on the overhead light in the kitchen. He answered a stale hello, his breath bouncing back at him.

"Is that you Sig, you dirty old bastard?"

"What a ya got for me, Shirley?"

Shirley was a barmaid downtown. Despite years of smoke-filled rooms and groping patrons, there was still a spark in her voice. "Some Blondie down here asking for a cab. Only lives over to Provincetown, name is Caroline."

"Okay, great, I'll be right over."

"Hey nice ad, you coming up in the world?"

"I'll still be there for you, sweet thing."

"Well, if you can fit your swelled head in the door, she's at the front table."

Sig went into the bathroom, splashed his face with the metallic water of Cape Cod, toweled off and headed out the door. He pulled a black suit jacket over his jeans and white shirt as he plodded down the stairs. He knew he'd be tired for one of his regular fares tomorrow, Mrs. Anthony's hair appointment, but he was looking for a way out of that bullshit anyway. Treated him like a personal chauffeur for ten bucks a ride, they did.

He pulled up into the well-lit parking lot still full of cars and heard the din coming from the July college kids, slinging shooters and slurring over the waitresses, their rich-kid Polo shirts stained with beer dribble. He slowed his Bonneville, black and beautiful, and pulled around toward the front door. He checked his look in the rearview mirror and saw his debuting bald spot highlighted as the interior light came on with the open passenger door.

"Are you my ride?" a blond woman asked him. She was around the age his daughter Amy would be, twenty-five maybe, in jeans and a white T-shirt, tucked in tight. Her right eye drifted slightly to the outside, the only indication to Sig that she had been drinking.

"You Caroline? Yeah, get in," Sig jutted his chin to the back.

She slammed the front door, and got in the back seat. "Nice car, I thought I called a cab though."

"No cabs in these parts, not enough business. I just started doing this on the side. Could have called one from Provincetown, but they'd rip you off for out-of-town fares. It's gonna be fifteen bucks, okay?"

"Yeah, okay, I just need to get home. I had a little too much." Sig saw her look out the side window, her profile delicate.

The fumes of her breath filled the car, the warmth of the liquor tingled the back of his tonsils. He pulled out of the driveway and headed for the long empty stretch of road between Wellfleet and Provincetown.

"Really tied one on, huh?" he asked.

"I don't even know what I'm doing up here, I just had to get out of P'town for the night."

"Girl trouble?"

"No." He could feel her looking at him in the rear view mirror. She's probably thinking "Whoa, hip dude, doesn't assume I'm straight. Interesting. Sexy."

"Actually it's boy trouble. My husband really."

"'Nother woman?"

"Well, kind of, I think he has a thing for his best friend. Who is a she," she rushed to add, a laugh almost. "She's pregnant," she said out the window.

"By him?"

"No, another guy, some jerk."

"So what's the problem?"

He could feel her searching the rearview mirror, trying to tease out eye contact. He turned his head over his shoulder and looked at her for a moment, then turned his attention back to the road.

"My husband loves this woman, I think. I don't think they're doing anything, which almost makes it worse. He wants to, I know, but he doesn't want to hurt me. It's weird."

"Husbands go through those kind of things."

"You married?"

"Was." Almost.

"Kids?"

"Just one." Sort of.

"You got anything to drink?"

Shit. He had a case of JD in the trunk, the stash he had bought off his buddy, a trucker.

"Yeah, but I don't drink on duty," he said trying to put her off although his head did feel heavy, unbalanced on his neck.

"Well here, I'll pay you now and you'll be off duty." She stuck her pelvis straight out and off the seat and jammed a tanned hand into her jeans pocket and pulled out a wad of money all crumpled and moist.

"Waitress," she said.

She counted out the money, exaggerated bank teller accuracy. She dropped four fives over the seat.

"Here, you're officially off duty," she said.

He drove another few seconds and then pulled over in the rest stop. He tried to allay any apprehension by explaining that the booze was in the trunk. Sad thing was she didn't even seem to realize that he was in a position to do whatever he goddamned wanted to.

He hauled himself out of the car and walked stiffly to the trunk and popped it. The case of booze lay virgin in his trunk, he hated to open it. He reached in and worked on the cardboard. Caroline's footsteps rustled their way into the woods, probably to take a piss. He saw the path of underbrush parting to make way for her. As she disappeared into the woods, the images of Mailin emerged from the deep forest of his mind.

Mailin would wait for him in the front room of her parent's hut. It was a low, small home, in one of the many low, small villages of Vietnam. Sig knew that they cleared out for him and Mailin to be alone, the inconvenience was considered an investment, a potential windfall, snagging an American husband. But he also knew that aside from whatever hopes Mailin had, she also loved him right in the moment. He couldn't get enough of making love to her, sweet and slow, he'd watch her respond. The hum of her quiet moans, her sweet silky hair washed in jasmine, the curtains that swayed a seductive dance. She would rub his head afterward as he nestled it between her small tight breasts, her fingers tracing the outline of his nose, eyes, the grooved maze of his ear. She saw into him, past the sun darkened fear, into the crackling optimism of a 19 year old American boy who never felt so on top of his game as when he entered that room, as when he entered her.

He fucked her mean only once, the time she told him she was pregnant. He was on top of her, ready, when she told him, and he instantly lost his erection, his interest. He accused her of trying to trap him, to trick him. She held onto his shoulders and tried to talk, her horrible broken baby English pleas. He knew she wasn't lying. A gray gritty swirl of dust filled his throat and stomach. He swallowed, his erection back, and without answering her questions, sealing her doom, he pushed himself into her, hard, her face full of tears and snot. When he was done pounding, he flipped on his back, leaving her on hers. They stared at the same water-stained ceiling, smelled the same stale oil of poverty. He looked down the length of her slim naked body and thought of their genetic mix resting unaware in Mailin's belly, quietly sucking her little nib of a thumb. He knew Mailin would make a good wife if that sweet sparkling eyedance of hers was any indication. Instead he ran scared, more scared of her than even the war somehow. He just stopped seeing her and when he was rotated out he hadn't looked back.

His youth, stalled by the war, seemed to run endlessly even now through his 50s. Coming home from Vietnam he found he missed Mailin, wondered about the baby, even made up the name Amy, just to have a name to put to it. To her. He thought sometimes of finding them and bringing them back, imagined them standing out so painful surrounded by all this good Yankee breeding.

Fuck. What was he doing back 25, 30 years ago? Ancient history. He set the bottle on the ground and straightened. He hunched up his wide shoulders to tuck in the tails of his shirt, grateful that his stomach was still so flat. He glanced onto the highway on the lookout for cops, but not a car passed. The tall pines swayed at drunken attention, as he listened for Caroline.

He heard her coming up from the woods. He slowly closed the lid of the trunk, easing out the small interior light that spotlighted under his chin. He ducked down, as she approached.

"I am back," she sang in a false scary voice, a laugh in her throat. She opened the front door. Sig heard the rush of air escape from the padded front seat as she sat. He could imagine her pushing her hair back behind her ear, waiting. He hoped someone had warned his daughter Amy not to do shit like this, not to put herself in situations where she could get hurt.

Sig's adrenaline rose, his heart started to sound too loud. He wiped his face, looked to the sky, his thumb and forefinger rested momentarily in the corners of his mouth, trying to clear his mind of this surge. Like a newsflash crossing the bottom of the screen his brain read: this is only a girl. A stupid innocent girl who doesn't even feel how close she is. Doesn't sense that he only has to reach out, one lunge, one irretrievable fluid motion.

"Hey, you out there?" she called to the woods. He held his position for a moment, crouched by the dirty license plate. He picked up the bottle and walked to the car door, leaving the outlined shadow of violence behind him, and got back into the driver's seat. The bright light of the moon flashed a lighthouse beam as a cloud passed over it. The night wind raised the underside of the leaves. He grabbed the clipboard and thermos by Caroline's feet and slid them into the back.

"Why don't we go down to the beach to drink this?" she asked, adjusting herself in the lighted vanity mirror on the visor. A second wind was in evidence, she was sparkly, animated, bright.

"Look, you're alone, drunk, with a bottle of JD between your legs and some guy old enough to be your father," he said, aware of blowing an already slim chance. "What if I was some psycho killer? Doesn't that worry you at all?"

She snapped the visor up, pulled on her seat belt and tried to insert it, metal buckles breaking the silence of the salt sea air swirling around them.

"Not particularly, weirdo," she said more to the windshield than to him.

They sailed through Truro and up and over the swells of Route 6 to reveal Provincetown, a serpent's tail curled out before them, lights sparkling into the sea. Caroline settled into the passenger seat, her window open, bottle clutched in one hand, resting on her thigh.

He could feel the whiskey clinging to his ribs, that first swallow of the night so greedily absorbed by the lining of his mouth, his tongue, a wonder there was enough left to swallow.

Sig tapped her hand, "Pass that would you?"

He could still feel the warmth of Caroline's hand on the square squat bottle. He missed that human contact, not just the sex which he craved more than ever, but the feel of someone close, that soft current that passes between the shoulders of a couple out for a drive, out on a night like this.

"My road's up here on the right, before you get to the airport," she said.

"I'll check it on the way back, maybe I'll pick up a fare."

She stared at her wristwatch for a moment, then said, "You should stop first, the last flight from Boston came in like five minutes ago."

"You don't mind?"

"The night is young."

He turned onto the dark road and drove surrounded by the scraggly pitchpine forest. The tiny airport parking lot was dark, a few cars on the side, employees' probably, one cab already. Sig capped the bottle and stowed it under his seat, fished through the ashtray filled with change for a stick of gum, uncurled the foil wrapper and popped in a piece.

"Looks empty," Caroline said.

Sig pulled up past the small terminal and around the parking lot to face the runway, wishing his sweet Bonneville could just take off over the cold black sea. He'd strap Mailin in tight and transport her back to that bed when she told him and he'd hug her tight and make plans. He had never even made plans with a woman, he realized.

"Neither of you have the heart for it," Caroline said, flashing him that killer profile again.

159

"You could do whatever you want to me. My husband can do whatever he wants with her. But really it's me that has it all. I could lean over to you now and suggest something nice and slow, or something mean and fast, and you'd do it either way, both of you would, poor fuckers." She pulled on her bitterness and sat low, wrapped in it.

"I can just take what you're holding back, don't you see that?" his intensity constricted his temples, his vision abnormally clear.

"But you won't. That's what I'm saying."

Sig ran his palm from his forehead up over his hair to rest in his baldspot nest. Since when did women talk this way? he thought, as he put the car in reverse. Mailin's eyedance skittered through his mind again; he poked under the seat until he felt the cool glass reassurance.

His car glided its way back down the road. Soon he'd be alone again. He'd drop Caroline back off into her heap of dirty life and she'd grope her way through the darkened hallways to find her bed either empty or full, her path determined by that. He'd wake up tomorrow morning and wait for Mrs. Anthony at her hair appointment, leaning the newspaper up against the steering wheel, sunglasses shading the glare of the bright sun in the small town puddles, a wave or a nod here and there to the occasional passersby.

The silty rawness of missed opportunity could be dismissed as indigestion, and he'd grope his own way into the evening's stillness. He'd drive to the ocean and get out of the car and gaze to the invisible horizon and feel the return gaze of Mailin thousands of miles away, and he'd feel the pull toward her as she turns her shoulder from the shore, and walks away, leaving him to drive back into his still, dusty life.

BARBARA MELCHER, "THE SCALLOPER"
ETCHING

Notes from a Poetry Workshop Instructor

BY JUNE BEISCH

You have an ability to generate ideas at
an alarming rate.

You run up to an idea, pinch it on the bottom
and then run away.

Caress the idea, and caress the detail.

These are really women's poems.
Try to focus on something other than yourself.

I like the musicality and the rhyme,
but where is the irony and ambiguity?

Emily Dickinson you're not.

These poems are too messagey.
What are these poems trying to say?

Poetry can fill the gaps within your life.
Poems are made of love not made.

Ghost: In The Garden

Emily Dickinson
1830–1886

BY JADENE FELINA STEVENS

I have tried to avoid you

to step politely around those
frigid spaces
you inhabit.

You smile nebulously
timid, but determined, as a wren.

It is only the cold drafts
which separate us, you whisper.

I can feel you, so often
as you peer over my shoulder
study the words

the black shadows on the white sheet

. . . contrast
you like contrast . . .

me, a dark-haired Italian of passion
my blood Mediterranean warm

you, the Belle of Amherst
quiet and self-contained
in your white habit

as you hover over my poems

. . . you flinch

a word too many

a word misplaced

the wrong word . . .

your fingers twitch.

You want to cross over again
but the ferryman refuses.

You set your lip . . .

sigh in the faint wind
that stirs tawny lily and prim daisy.

I can feel it
feel you concocting a plan

a way to get back
to your earthly words.

Now, when my hand writes
I feel your hand guiding it, sister . . .

a collaboration of spirits

outside of the fathers' heaven—

heaven in your own garden
in mine.

*One of a four-poem sequence which was awarded
Phi Theta Kappa's 1997 Nota Bene Citation Award*

Scrolling

BY JADENE FELINA STEVENS

Sappho speaks

the millennial winds swallow her words
we hear only fragments of her voice
her poems—

 exquisite fragments.

Sand scrapes ink from parchment
peels blackened words from the skin of reeds

yet

strips survive
wrapped around the body of a mummified cat
buried in an urn
in the desert . . .

we scroll through her words once again.

I want to bury a poem in my own Sahara—
the backside of the Provinceland Dunes—
see if anyone finds it
in a new millennium

see if anyone gingerly unrolls it
tongues the words

recalls me for a brief explanation . . .

and, once recalled, I may refuse to leave
the coarse, wild winds
the gathered warmth of the crushed quartz
the salt, the sea

I may quietly, passionately scratch
more words
sentence fragments
whole new poems

in the sand
on the backs of candy wrappers
paperbags, driftwood, shells

creating and recreating
tirelessly and without end

lost moments
worlds

priestess poets
sacred fat cats

temples where
ice water babbles
among the apple branches
and musk roses . . .

a cool summer oasis
love.

Note: The words in italics were surviving fragments of a poem
by Sappho, Aeolic Greek poet 630-570 B.C.

The Ecstacy of Marian Wicker

BY J. LORRAINE BROWN

MARIAN WICKER HAD THIS THING ABOUT SMELLS. Odors hung in the air like kites. They floated round and round in her head like tunes she couldn't name, distracting her so much she was unable to focus on anything else.

The first time it happened, it was a Sunday afternoon. Marian was sitting in the living room, gazing out the window, counting the hours until she could go to bed. Marian hated passing time. She had to grip each hour with both hands and yank it minute by minute in a tedious game of tug o' war. Now Marian wrinkled her nose and sniffed gently. She got up from the couch, her head high, her nose still sniffing, and walked deliberately through the kitchen, into the dining room, down the front hall, and back into the kitchen. The odor sat on the tip of her tongue until she finally decided it must be cabbage from the corned beef dinner she had cooked several nights ago. Marian burned candles after frying liver or boiling cabbage. Her favorite scent was gardenia. Maybe I didn't burn them long enough, she thought, and she opened the window over the sink to let in some fresh air.

Marian lived alone and didn't like it one bit. Most of her friends had either died or moved to Florida, and she often wondered why people gave going-away parties when it was the ones left behind who needed cheering up. Lila Kane, her best friend, was the last to leave, and in the beginning her letters arrived in a haphazard but faithful fashion. They stuck out of the black mailbox inside Marian's small front porch, and she found herself listening for the scrape of the lid announcing the mailman.

Lila's letters reminded her of the serials she enjoyed in the Jason Theater when she was young and admission only fifteen cents. She waited impatiently for the next installment. Lila's letters ceased eventually, and Marian had only herself to blame. She was a poor correspondent. Boxes of unused stationery jammed her desk drawers, different pictures showing through their clear covers. A still life of flowers would catch her eye or a scene by Van Gogh or Matisse, and Marian bought the box. Instead of tempting her to write, it nagged her until she stashed it out of sight.

"You have to write a letter to receive a letter," Eileen said whenever Marian complained she never heard from anyone anymore, but each time she sat down at her desk, her mind went as blank as the empty page in front of her. Friendships dried up, shrinking to a few scribbled words on a Christmas card and disappearing when there were no words at all.

She tried using the telephone.

"Please leave a message, and we will . . ."

"Pooh!" She replaced the receiver, cutting off the recording she knew by heart. No one was ever home when she called, and what was the point of talking to an answering machine.

"I need to talk when I want to talk," she said.

She wished she still had her driver's license, but she had to give it up. Road signs became pedestrians, and one night in the dusk, a bush alongside the highway crouched like an old dog and made her slam on her brakes. Marian decided then to drive only in the daytime and only if the sun wasn't bright enough to bounce off her glasses.

It wasn't enough. Too many times she couldn't find the library. Too many times the supermarket wasn't where it was supposed to be. On those days, she had driven around for what seemed like hours, trying to recognize street names, panic rising in her chest like water. What if one day, she couldn't find her way back home? Then in the car wash, she stepped on the gas instead of the brake and bumped into a wall. It could have happened to anyone, a little lump on the forehead, but the owner made a big deal of it. He sent for an ambulance even though Marian assured him she was fine. All she needed was an ice pack in her own kitchen. The worst of it was the local paper printed the details of her accident along with her age for all the world to see. She let her license lapse. She told the children her reflexes were too slow, and she kept her fears a secret.

"Are you sure?" they said.

"I'll take the bus if I have to," she said, "or a taxi."

Marian wanted to live with one of her children. If I ask, she told herself, it won't be the same. She waited for them to read her mind, but they visited her instead, making tea and sitting for an hour or so as though, Marian thought, she were a duty to be discharged. When Marian hinted she was lonesome, they invited her to dinner. When she mentioned the house was getting too big for her, they hired a cleaning lady. And when she worried about burglars, they put in an alarm system.

The next time Marian noticed the smell, it seemed to be coming from the sunroom. She was searching under pillows, trying to locate the source, when Eileen arrived.

"Over here," she said to her daughter who had stopped by for a quick visit on her way to somewhere else. Eileen was always so busy, running here and there, involved in this and that, and Marian thought that all of her visits were too quick. Eileen took off her coat and hung it over the back of a kitchen chair.

"What are you talking about, Mother?" she said. "Everything's fine. I can't stay too long. I'm meeting Roger at five o'clock. We're driving to Cambridge to meet Ken and Grace for dinner. It's their anniversary."

"Here, lean over and smell. Something sour. It's been driving me crazy. Why can't you smell it?"

Eileen sighed and inhaled the air in front of her. "I really don't smell anything, Mother," she said. "And I have a good nose."

"Well, how can I argue with that," Marian said.

For once, Marian could hardly wait for Eileen to leave. She was that anxious to tear the room apart. But all her efforts revealed nothing. She pulled all the cushions off the couch and examined them front and back. She dragged the couch away from the wall and on her hands and knees checked behind it. She lifted up the rug. Not even a dust ball, but then Marian was the kind of woman who made her bed first thing, who never came downstairs until she was dressed, who organized her closets. It was unthinkable such a bad smell could be in her house, but there definitely was an odor, and it made her burn with embarrassment to think that she was slipping.

She admitted to herself afterwards Eileen might have been the wrong person to ask. Eileen didn't take the time to pay attention, but what if someone else had dropped by? What if it had been Anita Corby?

Marian remembered the day Anita moved in across the street. The moving van wasn't gone but a few hours when she saw Anita outside on a ladder cleaning out the drains. She was that efficient. She wrapped her artificial Christmas tree in plastic, ornaments still in place, and planted it in her basement already decorated and ready for next year. Whatever would Anita think if she dropped by for a cup of coffee and a chat? But that time, as fast as it came, the smell disappeared, leaving her dizzy with the sheer relief of it.

Michael would have been the better choice, she thought, so the next time she saw Michael, she mentioned it to him. "It comes and goes," she said.

"Well, I don't smell anything now, Mom," he said. "It could be mice. Maybe there's a dead one trapped somewhere. I could call an exterminator if you want."

"I don't think it's mice," said Marian. "I would have heard them. You know it's really quiet here with just me all by myself."

"It's up to you then." Michael retreated behind his newspaper. "But I wouldn't worry about it. It can't be all that bad if you don't smell it all the time." Marian decided not to mention the subject to anyone again.

When it returned the next time, she tracked it once more into the kitchen. It must be something in the fridge, she thought. She opened every Tupperware container and sniffed, and the only offensive thing she found was a potato as brown and wrinkled as an old face. Marian pounced on it gleefully. At last! She dropped it with a thud in the garbage bin. She washed each shelf carefully with soapy water, replacing the box of baking soda just in case. She took all the spice jars out of the cabinet and wiped them with a damp rag. She washed the counters, rinsing the dishcloth over and over again until her hands were pruney and the counters gleamed.

The smell returned the next day. The minute she opened her eyes in the morning, she knew it was back. It's everywhere I am. It must be me, she thought. She threw back the quilt and dropped her legs over the side of the bed. Her skin hung from the bones of her arms, white and loose and billowy, like sheets on a line, and Marian pressed her face into her arm and took a deep breath. She hoisted herself out of bed and padded into the bathroom. She turned the taps on full force and dropped pale yellow beads filled with perfume into the tub. Then she lay back in the water. She remembered telling Eileen about Ivan at the beauty parlor. How he had bowed gallantly and reached for her hand to lead her to his station. "He's very attentive to me," she said.

"That's nice, mother," Eileen replied.

I am a foolish old woman, Marian thought, and she soaked until the beads disappeared.

The smell was constant now, a refrain in the background like elevator music. Marian found it almost impossible to separate food smells from the unpleasant odor. She began to sneak up on her meals, snatching quick little bites. She sipped slowly between breaths. She lost weight. Her skin felt sticky like wax. I am melting, she thought. Bit by bit pieces of her were sliding away, and she wondered what would be left of her in the end.

"You need to get out more, Mother. Let's go to lunch," and Marian could see the concern lining Eileen's face, making her look old, but she declined every time. The thought of eating made her gag. She felt better if she stayed home and cleaned. "First things first," she said.

When Marian was a young girl, her mother repeated that phrase like a mantra: *Clean your room, Marian. First things first and then you can do whatever you want with your day.* It was a habit that hardened like cement until Marian never had to make a conscious choice. She did her chores, her homework. She ironed her husband's shirts, folded clothes, emptied ashtrays, wiped counters and dirty little faces. I'll just do this and this and this. Like a string of rosary beads, she counted off her duties one by one, and only then did she earn the right to relax.

First things first, she whispered over and over when all she really wanted to do was fall asleep. The only time she wasn't aware of the smell was at night when she slept. She closed her eyes, and when she opened them again, she was on a dusty path in the middle of a field, a flat, flat field stretching as far as her eye could see with ribbons of frayed, dusty road intersecting it like twine. Marian walked along the paths. The air was fresh and clover-scented, and breezes rippled her hair.

She began taking naps during the day, but today she couldn't fall asleep, and today was the worst day ever. The stench layered the air, dense and miasmic, forcing her to hold her breath until she felt faint. She sat by the window and watched as rain bounced off the pavement outside.

Drops hit the ground and bounced back up again. They pooled in green wavery puddles in the driveway where her car used to be. They hung from the trees, long, fat drops, hanging on until the very last minute, finally letting go and sliding into the grass.

Everything looked cool and delicious, and Marian slipped off her housecoat and let it fall to the floor. She lifted her nightgown over her head and stepped out of her slippers. When she opened the front door, a gush of warm, sweet air wrapped itself around her and pulled her outside, down the brick steps, and into the yard. She stood silent in the grass. She raised her arms and let the water run down her skin and carry away the smell.

This story was previously published in Willow Review, *College of Lake County Publications, Spring 2002.*

Legacies

BY ELIZABETH SWANSON GOLDBERG

Reaching the bottom tray of the safebox
she grasps a rough triangle
tucked in a bit of tissue,
cups it in the palm of her hand.
Allows her daughter to stroke it; says,
when I was in school I took biology
and chemistry and anatomy, and I loved
science and medicine and healing, and
we dissected this cat. This is her ear.
I could not be a doctor, but
you can be what you want to be.
And the little girl thinks of creatures
who died so that others could move
about the world and grow.
And of the silence of her mother's hands,
which had not moved over bodies for their healing.

And later she will think of the silences
where some women are not anymore,
moving as they have into light, motion, voice.
Silences passed from those for whose sound
others laid themselves down,
who jar the air with the smugness of "I'm free"
and tie the tongues of those who are not,
ensuring they will never be.

And she will hear the silences
where women are still not,
lodged as they are in corners and kitchens,
moving as they do into death.
The clamor of these quiets chafes:

it is stillness jammed tight and throbbing,
not like simple vibrations moving air
but rather pressure clotting the breath,
a nervous thickening of the atmosphere.

And the quiet loss of two able hands on some surgical team
will roar for her to thunder, inflamed by this whine which,
    having achieved voice,
drowns out the history of silence so as to secure its eternal life.

EDITH VONNEGUT,
"HANGING THE LAUNDRY"
OIL ON CANVAS

Life Drawing

BY CANDACE PERRY

"AND DON'T FORGET MY CIGARETTES," Luke's mother calls out to him. "I'm gonna switch to them Lady Eves if you don't quit takin' my Winstons. You'll look mighty limp in the wrist puffin' a butt with flowers on it!"

"Yeah, yeah," Luke answers on his way out, reminded again that he needs to fix the storm door as it rattles in the wind. He has to wait for the car's engine to warm up, or it'll go dead on him at the first stop sign. From the curb he sees the blue light of the television flickering on the living room ceiling, sees smoke from his mother's cigarette rise, reflecting blue. He can't see her, but he knows she is sitting on the edge of the plaid sofa, motionless until the ash of her Winston seems bound to drop. Like a statue, not really watching the TV, but looking beyond it.

He wishes she'd just let up about replacing that goddamned pack of Winstons he'd borrowed. Since he'd graduated high school three years ago she'd been like that. "I ain't bustin' my butt takin' every odd job I can find to keep a roof over my head so I can keep supportin' you, mister." Seven a.m., the morning after graduation, he'd only been in bed an hour or so, she's ripping the covers off of him. "I mean it, Luke, get up or get out." The end of every week now she had a bill for him for his half, like he was a boarder instead of her only child. Maybe this is the year he'll move out, except on account of the college all the apartments in town are overpriced.

He doesn't hold it against his mother that she squeezes every nickel. Life hasn't dealt her the best hand. He knows she dropped out of high school to have him, even though she'll never admit that pregnancy, not true love, was the reason for his father's marriage to her. Luke can't tell if his vague memories of the man are from real events or just photographs. He left them when Luke was two, went out for cigarettes and never came back. His mother still wears her wedding band, some proof she's not white trash. "Sure am glad he left us your good looks," she says to Luke every chance she gets.

Even in old photographs when she was dressed up she was no beauty. After all these years as a smoker her face has a pinched, gray look to it, like she'd been inhaling too hard through the filtered Winstons she'd switched to after a coughing fit she had all through his Sophomore year. She's still vain about her figure though, won't let him bring any Fritos or Twinkies into the house.

He worries about her, wishes he could make enough to support them both, or at least so she wouldn't have to take every crummy job she can find. Since Christmas she's been working every Thursday night at the college. All she'll say is she's going up to the college, which Luke knows to mean she's taken a cleaning job again. He doesn't like to think of that, of her as a cleaning woman to the snotty rich kids who drop their cafe latte cups wherever they damn well please.

A handful of local kids got scholarships to the college, but Luke wasn't one, hadn't even tried. In high school he and his friends had made fun of the geeks and nerds at the college, but now Luke notices what good cars most of them drive and how they dress like people in beer commercials. The Copy Center where Luke works caters to the college crowd, and he observes that even the ones who try to look scruffy still look rich. A piece of jewelry, an expensive hair cut, the Jeep they leave idling in the No Parking zone—some sign of their privilege always gives them away. Some of them are real jerks, like the fraternity boys who demanded fifteen collated copies of the *Sports Illustrated* swimwear issue five minutes before closing one night. Worse than the jerks are the do-gooders, girls always, who after asking questions that are none of their damn business, insist he should be in college, and somehow, even if they're Economics majors, don't believe he can't afford it.

Most of the student conversations Luke overhears at work have to do with getting wasted or laid, accomplishments he has no trouble managing without incurring debts he could never repay. He had to laugh when *U.S. News and World Report* labeled the college one of their "best buys." At $17,000 a year, forget about it.

Luke was recently made Night Manager of the Copy Center, an honor that only means he's the last one to leave work. His boss, the Colonel, owns four other Copy Centers in that part of southeastern Ohio which might as well be West Virginia. The Colonel is always telling Luke how he could go places in this company, but the places to go are all just like Luke's hometown: small and dull with overpriced liberal arts colleges to put them on the map. Luke envies the Colonel. When he was Luke's age, World War II came along, made him a pilot, gave him a military career and rewarded him with a retirement income that he parleyed into a decent business.

The military doesn't offer that kind of deal anymore. Smart boy like you oughta get an education, the Colonel is always saying, but Luke doesn't notice him handing out any $17,000 scholarships.

Business is slow this particular Monday night. The wind roars outside and a wet snow clings to the hats and shoulders of the few students who come in. Luke thinks of closing early, but the Colonel is a stickler about hours, insisting they're open for business until twenty-one hundred hours. Besides, all he has to do is go to the Quick Stop for cigarettes for his mom, nothing much happening in town. Closing up, he notices someone left their backpack. He doesn't exactly trust the kid who comes on in the morning, too likely to fish around looking for more than an ID in the wallet. The girl who owns the backpack is the kind who filled out the identification tag inside the L.L. Bean bag. A Kara Whitman, in Hunter Hall. He tries a couple of times to call her, but the line is busy, so he decides just to drop it off on his way home.

He knocks, and she opens the door to her room only partly. "Yes? Can I help you," she says and tucks a strand of dark hair back behind her ear.

Luke holds out the backpack, says, "You left this at the Copy Center. I've been trying to call to tell you."

"Oh my god, oh thank you, thank you. God, I didn't even realize I left it. I've been on the Net all night doing my taxes." Christ, it's only February. He likes how her hair falls over her face when she reaches her hand out to shake his. "I'm Kara, of course you knew that," and she nods nervously towards the backpack.

"Luke," he says.

"Nice to meet you, Luke. Thank you so much." She holds on to the "so," in a way that seems sincere on her, though he usually thinks it's phoney when other college girls use it. She strikes him as the kind of girl who doesn't know how pretty she is. They small-talk the miserable weather, the notes she would have missed come 2 a.m. when she started studying, how much she appreciates him going to the trouble. For a few minutes there, he's thinking she's different, but then she takes out her wallet and opens the part that holds the bills. Why didn't she just come out and say, Hey, townie, how much did you take?

"It's all there," he says.

She drops the backpack and reaches out to touch his arm. "Oh my god, I'm so sorry. I didn't mean, I mean I wasn't looking, I only wanted, oh shit, I can't get this right!" She pulls a ten dollar bill out of the wallet, takes in a breath. "What I was trying to do was thank you. Here, please take this."

Jesus Christ, what a piece of work. "Where I come from people just say thanks," he says and walks away as fast as he can.

"Well, where I come from people are assholes," Kara calls after him, and he turns back.

"You're welcome," he says, a slight smile cracking in spite of himself.

She holds up the bill. "Couldn't you let me buy you a beer, at least?"

Luke had never been in the Rathskeller in the Student Union basement, but he's glad she suggested it so they don't have to use his car to go someplace off campus. Damn thing would take forever to heat in this cold, plus the whole front seat was decorated with fast food wrappers and empty cigarette packs. She doesn't mind if he smokes, even tells him that after two beers she'll start trying to bum one from him and he's to refuse.

"I'm quitting," she says, "but I do love second hand smoke." When Kara goes to the ladies room she comes back with a fresh pack of Winstons. "Now you'll have to think of me every time you light up," she says, smiling as she hands them to him. Next time we go out I'll have to tell her not to do that. He doesn't say he'd be giving this pack to his mom since he owes her, and he doesn't say he'll need no reminders to think of Kara.

Luke can't remember having such a good time with a girl. She doesn't seem to care that he isn't in college. When he said he was too old for it, that if he started next year he'd be twenty-five by the time he got a degree, she said, "Well, in four years you'll be twenty-five whether you get a degree or not," and left it at that.

She's majoring in something called "Art History," because she isn't a good enough artist, she says, but her favorite class is Life Drawing.

"How do you draw life?" Luke asks, more relaxed now, after his third beer. In this bar you could actually talk, not like the places he usually goes where the television tries to drown out the dart players and the married guys hitting on the single moms.

"Life drawing is drawing the human body, nude, of course," Kara explains.

"Naked?" Luke asks, not hiding his surprise.

"Yep, naked nudes."

"Geez, my whole senior year we tried to convince the school board to let the school nurse give out condoms, and you'd think we were suggesting public orgies. Do they know you have naked people posing up there?"

"Don't tell," she laughs.

"So these naked people—"

"Nudes," she corrects.

"Okay, these nudes, are they men or women?"

"A man on Tuesday nights, woman on Thursday."

Luke is reminded of the first time he looked into a microscope in junior high, they'd examined a simple drop of water and it was full of such activity he'd never imagined. Who would have thought there were naked people standing around in classrooms in the old brick buildings of the college? He leans across the table, so he can whisper. "What happens when the guy gets a hard-on?"

"Luke!" Kara mocks a prudish surprise, insists she never looks. Then she turns more serious, telling him how really beautiful the human body is, and her face just lights up talking about art and what it's like to try to translate onto paper what you see with your eyes, feel in your heart. Luke listens, happy for her company.

When they notice they're the last people in the place, Kara asks Luke if he wants to go back to her place to see her etchings.

"What exactly does that mean, 'see your etchings'?"

"It means come back to my place. The etchings are just an excuse."

They hold hands as they run across the snow-covered quad. Her room is small, a single, so no roommate to worry about. The walls are covered with her drawings and paintings. Luke doesn't know anything about art, but he figures he has to say something. He points out a painting of a bright wheat field, with dark birds, maybe crows, in the sky. "This is really great, kind of crazy cheerful, but sad."

"It's just a copy I did of a Van Gogh. I wanted to see what it felt like to paint it. It was his last work before he killed himself."

"You're not cutting off your ear, too, are you? Seems you'd be at a loss for where to put that strand of hair." Gently, he reaches for her, and she turns out the lights.

Afterwards, they share a cigarette. He tells her about bumming from his mom, what she'd said that night about switching to Lady Eves if he didn't quit smoking hers.

"Your mom sounds like someone I'd like to meet," Kara says.

Why not, Luke thinks. Something truly wonderful is happening here. She understands that he has to go home, that his mother would worry if he didn't. Kara is smiling when he goes into the bathroom to wash up. He closes the door behind him. Taped to the door is a drawing of a woman, a nude with sagging breasts and a hard face. He's afraid he might throw up.

"Where'd you get this picture?" he opens the door, motions to the back of it.

"I did that in my Thursday night class." Kara is stretched out on her bed, her perfect breasts catching the light from the bathroom. "I think it's the best thing I've done, but whenever my mother visits she tacks a washcloth over the body. She says it's disgusting, but she doesn't know anything about art."

Luke closes the bathroom door, runs water in the sink. He takes Kara's drawing of his mother off the door and tears it into small pieces which he flushes down the toilet.

COCO LARRAIN, "THE INVITATION," CHARCOAL DRAWING

I violate . . .

BY NANCY "DING" WATSON

I violate
with a knife
a clam's stubbornly held
fortress of shell
while his brothers
whistle in my sink

one by one my
blade enters their temples
and destroys the will
lying in each muscle
holding together with
such apparent conviction
a life
until I come to the last clam
I have tried him and
returned him to the pile
three times
he is defending something here
now I would conquer this last clam
this blade of mine would slice his
fresh glistening muscle
neatly in half
I would feel the
twin curved walls
slacken and fall to my
skill and superior wisdom

what happens then is
a colossal
failure of will on my part
I cannot open the clam

I meditate
chin in hand
staring out the window at the
birds fluttering about the feeder
then I go back and
catch the clam
and myself
unawares
or has he felt that I would
have to spare him
and so relaxed his grip
or has he smelled the
death of his brothers
and given up hope
who knows
at any rate my knife
dives inside and
sharpens wickedly on
tender meat

now I do not want to eat them
but I cannot see
throwing away a whole bowlful
of sweet salt juice and
soft bodies
I am after all hungry
and poor
nature dictates that I should
eat the clams
plus which
I have killed them
I have to pay the price

I begin peeling the potatoes
for the chowder

The sea crashes . . .

BY NANCY "DING" WATSON

The sea crashes

beneath my Truro dune
the boom reverberates
and I climb to the top to observe

far below
three endless rows of breakers
beat against the sand
and out where the boats
curve about the horizon
the white caps roil and the
wind dashes the sea gulls into
long swoops

I watch and remember
being out there in the white foam
lost in gigantic storms between
Portugal and home
full of fear that you will be
swept overboard
swallowed like a bit of weed in
thick and violent swells while I
balance on the wet deck
trying to spot you in the
sucking waves and walls of wind

I could get home without you
that is not my fear
it's that I would get home
without you

tomorrow we will go aboard
pull up our anchor hung with

mysterious weed and strange
pulsing fauna
we'll brace our bodies against the gods
as though defying an angry father
and I will pray
if not to Poseidon then to any god
(laughing at Homer may be okay but
laughing at other people's gods is
dangerous business
supposing they should hear)

we'll smile at each other at

light of day and
weave our bodies tightly together in the
narrow bunk at night
and the gods will
do their thing

LIZ PERRY, "SCALLOPS," MONOPRINT

Sunset Glow

BY RACHEL ELLIS KAUFMAN

I left Home so long ago!
In search of beauty first,
Of love, adventure—
To get acquainted with the truth of things.

Questing for what?
I didn't know, but—
Life's mysteries drew me on;
They beckoned and I followed.

Was it Art that I was after?
Poetry?
The urge to create was upon me—
Yet to create exactly what?
(How could I know that I was creating
Myself?)

So I painted pictures and I wrote poems
And I saw that they were good—for their day.
But then times changed, becoming "Post-Modern"
(As if it isn't always "now"!)

My creations went out of style.
Poetry went out of rhyme.
Meter became cadence
And "Beauty" became a dirty word!

I began to see the world as changed,
No longer beautiful, mysterious or fulfilling.
I saw that I had been where I was going . . .
I thought of Home.

Isn't that where we belong at life's close?
Among the other older ones—

Old friends, and old relations
Old towns and simple village Main Streets—
Treading pathways through the woods and fields.

Pausing to gaze again at old, familiar vistas.
The mountains, deserts, oceans of our youth
Gaze back at us again in "Welcome Home!"

So here I is, at Home once more,
And home again to stay!
I paint again, and sing.
Creation gushes forth—
The fruit of what I had to learn abroad.

Is Home a place for rest?
It's yes, and no—
A place to culminate, to gather in the crops
Development is done, and done the days of growth,
The struggle to attain.

We are enlarged by life, the very living of it
I have become a setting sun
Bathed in my own sunset glow.
Who knows where I shall rise again?

—RACHEL ELLIS KAUFMAN, MARCH 18, 1999

Fort Hill

BY ELINOR GELSEY

1.

Clear as a clarion call
the view from the hill.
Cedar-rimmed, meadows slope,
   stone-walled,
      spill
         into the marsh,
all curves and sinewy waterways.

Sun-lapped, green grasses fade
   into fawn, rustle the grays
      of glacial stones that
scatter the shore.

The wind sighs, the sea answers.
   A rondeau.

2.

Did they stand here, gaze
toward the east—
those People of the First Light?

Did they scan the sea, eyes
keen as the sharp-shinned hawk?

Did they run, swift as the red fox,
along the path to Skiff Hill
and the Sharpening Stone?
Even as they honed the double edge
of their arrowheads, ships hove

into view. Did Kiehtan speak?
Did Crow call a warning?
The locust sang of the White Frost
and a chill deeper than winter.

Tisquantum.
Samoset.
Massasoit.
Wamsutta.

Names like a drum roll.

Author Biographies

MARGUERITE AHLBERG
Marguerite Ahlberg left the mountains of Pennsylvania to come to sea level on Cape Cod. She taught language arts in elementary school. She writes more journals and essays than poetry, and has had some of her work published in *The Cape Codder* and *Prime Time*. She has belonged to the Wellfleet Writers, Salt Wind Poets, and the Brewster Poetry Workshop.

KARRI ANN ALLRICH
Karri Ann Allrich is an artist, cook and author. She shares her Brewster home and studio with her artist/author husband, Steve Allrich, and their two strapping sons. Her new and forthcoming titles include *A Witch's Book of Dreams, Cooking by Moonlight*, and *Cooking by the Seasons*.

JUNE BEISCH
June Beisch teaches American literature at Emerson College and at Mass. Bay Community College in Wellesley. Her essay "The Wolf" was named a "notable essay of 1998" by Robert Atwan. Her recent fiction appears in *The Literary Review* and *The Charles River Review*, and she is a Poet in the Schools in Stoneham, Mass. She divides her time between Cambridge and Chatham.

MARILYN BENTOV
Marilyn Bentov has studied religion, philosophy, media and performing arts, and received her doctorate in 1973 from Harvard University. She has worked as a writer, producer, director, workshop designer, group leader, and storyteller. Her poetry on Cape Cod reflects glorious days spent in a dune cottage on Eastham Bay.

LESLIE BRETT
Leslie Brett has published poems in the *Clackamas Literary Review* and *The Seattle Literary Review*, and her poems won second prize in *CapeWomen* magazine's 2000 Annual Poetry Contest. She lives in West Hartford, Connecticut, and also shares a home in Truro with her partner and two friends. She is the Executive Director of the Connecticut Permanent Commission on the Status of Women.

CELIA BROWN
Celia Brown is a Cape Cod resident who grew up in Ireland. A former nurse, she holds degrees from New England College and Dartmouth College. She has been in writing fellowships and published in many journals. She has read poetry at the Library of Congress, and her book, *Mending the Skies,* was published by Fithian Press in 2000. Some of her poems about nursing are forthcoming in an anthology called *Intensive Care,* to be published in 2003 by The University of Iowa Press.

LORRAINE BROWN
J. Lorraine Brown is a full-time writer and received a Massachusetts Cultural Council Professional Development Grant in 2001. "The Ecstasy of Marian Wicker" was previously published in the Spring 2002 issue of *Willow Review*. Her work has also appeared or is forthcoming in *Tulane Review, The South Carolina Review, Descant, Red Wheelbarrow, Lumina, The Pegasus Review, Potpourri* and *Phantasmagoria*.

LETTIE COWDEN

Lettie Cowden divides her time between Boca Raton, Florida, and Provincetown. She says, "Credit for my work goes to my friend Norman Mailer, and once upon a time my raving sweet Harry Kemp! They urged me to dance my wild dances, too, finding poetry in both the body and the soul. How more honored can I be?"

MARY DOERING

Mary Doering, a poet and artist from Orleans, graduated with honors from Lesley College with a degree in art therapy. She has won numerous awards for both her painting and poetry, including *CapeWomen* magazine's Annual Poetry Contest in 2000.

ANNE GARTON

Anne Garton is the Fiction and Poetry Editor of *CapeWomen* magazine and served for several years as the coordinator of "In Her Own Words," a fiction and poetry event sponsored by the Cape Cod Women's Organization. She is a former TV producer and has served as Project Director at WGBH's "Ready to Learn" children's TV initiative. Virginia Woolf is the subject of her Ph.D. dissertation and she has delivered academic papers at several universities, as well as lectured on Irish poetry at local bookstores. She is an avid culinary herbalist with extensive herb gardens, and owns a business in Eastham called Cottage Industry, specializing in rustic cottage-style antiques and collectibles.

GERRY DI GESU

Gerry di Gesu divides her time between Chatham and New Jersey. Her essays have been published in various publications, including *CapeWomen* magazine. She says, "The Cape is my refuge where the beauty and order in nature help bring balance and perspective to my writing. I believe in the inherent goodness of man and that even on the darkest days, there is a ray of hope to be found."

ELIZABETH SWANSON GOLDBERG

Elizabeth Swanson Goldberg, Ph.D., is Assistant Professor of Postcolonial Literature at Babson College, Wellesley, MA. She began writing poetry at the age of six, and continues to write and publish poems and critical essays. A native New Yorker, she has been deeply rooted in the sands of Cape Cod for the past eight years, and hopes to remain here for . . . ever.

JENNIFER GOSTIN

Jennifer Gostin's fiction often reflects her interest in the supernatural and folklore. Her stories have appeared in several journals, and her first novel, *Peregrine's Rest*, was published in 1996 by Permanent Press. She and her husband live in Eastham, where she's completed her second novel and is writing her third.

ROSE GOTSIS

Rose Gotsis is Senior Editor of the Longfellow Society Journal, a journal of poetry and prose. She has received three awards from The New England Anthology of Writers and has placed in the top three awards given by the Manuscript Club of Boston six different years. She writes for the *Metro West Daily News*, and her poetry, short stories, and articles have appeared in many literary magazines and national publications.

EDWINA GRAYSON
Edwina Grayson has a B.S. in education from Lesley College and has studied painting with Adolph Conrad and Stuart Kaufman in New Jersey. She studied at the Art Students' League in New York, has had many exhibitions of her art work in New York and New Jersey, and is the winner of several awards. She has published three books of poetry, *A Twilight Sky, Seeds to the Wind*, and *Moonraker*. She lives in New Jersey and summers in Truro.

JEBBA HANDLEY
Jebba Handley is both a fiction and nonfiction writer. Her stories have appeared or are forthcoming in *Baltimore Review, Larcom Review, Controlled Burn, Pangolin Papers, Ellipsis* and *Writers' Forum*. She also writes a bi-weekly column for *The Cape Codder* newspaper, "At Jebba's Table," on food, wine and the delights of entertaining at home. Writing is her full-time profession and she is at work on her first novel. "There is nothing I would rather be doing," she says.

GAYLE HEASLIP
Gayle Heaslip has lived on the Cape, raising a family, for over 25 years. She finds that the landscape has influenced her writing in the way its simple visual lines of earth, sea and sky are affected by the changing light, much as the ordinariness of what one calls "home" is experienced as emotional shades and textures. She is a photographer and seminary student and lives in Falmouth.

ROSEMARY HILLARD
Rosemary Hillard, taxi driver (Cape Cab)/poet/artist/art therapist/counselor and philosopher, lives and works in Provincetown. Her poetry has appeared in *We Are All Friends Here: An Anthology of Provincetown Poets, Provincetown Magazine, Poetry in your Face*, and *Provincetown Haiku*.

CYNTHIA HUNTINGTON
Cynthia Huntington's newest poetry collection, *The Radiant*, won the 2001 Levis Prize from Four Way Books, and will be published in 2003. She is the author of two previous award-winning books of poetry, *The Fish-Wife*, and *We Have Gone to the Beach*, as well as an acclaimed memoir, *The Salt House*. Huntington is the recipient of grants from the New Hampshire State Council on the Arts, the Fine Arts Work Center in Provincetown, and the Massachusetts Cultural Council, as well as two fellowships from the National Endowment for the Arts. She directs the Program in Creative Writing at Dartmouth College.

JAMIA KELLY
Jamie Kelly washed ashore in Provincetown in 1995. She has been writing poetry since 1958, and has published one volume, *Earthsong, Womansong*.

KRISTIN KNOWLES
Kristin Knowles grew up on Cape Cod and has been writing poetry since the age of 17. Still trying to emancipate herself from the restaurant business, she is a freelance writer, performance poet, and the Poetry Editor for *The Cape Codder* newspaper. In 1997, she won the Northeast Regional Performance Poetry Showcase and has represented Cape Cod at three National Poetry Slam competitions. She currently organizes performance poetry events all over Cape Cod and has had her poetry published in *CapeWomen* magazine.

Anne D. LeClaire
Chatham resident Anne D. LeClaire is a novelist and essayist who teaches creative writing on Cape Cod and in Jamaica. She is the author of many novels, including *Entering Normal;* her most recent book is *Leaving Eden* (Ballantine Books, September 2002). She is currently at work on another novel, *A Perfect Match*, and a nonfiction work on the practice of silence, *Stone Falling Through Silence.*

Wendy Levine
Wendy Levine is a writer and former psychotherapist who lives in Truro and Manhattan with her husband Kent. Her short stories, counseling columns and feature articles have appeared in many publications including *Woman's Life, Going Down Swinging, People and Places, Manhattan East*, and *CapeWomen*. Her short plays and children's musicals have been produced off-Broadway and two short plays were recently produced in Provincetown. She was a researcher and writer for Reader's Digest General Books and Producer of the Great Neck Community Theatre in Great Neck, NY. She serves on the Board of the Truro Center for The Arts at Castle Hill, where she established the Sabina Teichman Chair in honor of her mother, the painter Sabina Teichman.

Rena Lindstrom
Rena Lindstrom, from North Carolina, washed ashore in Provincetown about ten years ago, crisply burnt from the regulated professional life. She thanks the gods and goddesses for that happy accident, or was it fate? Whatever, she thrives here, rising every morning to be her self, another passenger on the runaway bus of a creative life. She's an artist and writer, mother, mate, friend, community member, worker, and a citizen in resistance to the imperialist US government.

Ruth Littlefield
Ruth V. Littlefield was born eighty-four years ago in Provincetown in the house she currently lives in. Her parents were also born in Provincetown. She left town for thirty five years after marrying and returned after the loss of her husband. She notes, "I love Provincetown and can't think of a place I would rather be."

Jacqueline M. Loring
Jacqueline M. Loring is a poet, writer and photographer who lives on the west side of Cape Cod with her large, blended family. Married to a Vietnam veteran since 1969, her poetry brings to the reader and listener thoughts about surviving the aftermath of war. She is a member of the National League of American Pen Women, and has had poems published in numerous journals and magazines. She is the editor of *Summer Home Review: An Anthology of Selected Poems and Stories.*

Suzanne McConnell
Suzanne McConnell's first novel, *Fence of Earth,* placed as a finalist for the James Fellowship for Novel in Progress, and is currently being submitted to publishers. She has published short stories, poetry, and nonfiction, including articles in recent issues of *CapeWomen* magazine. She teaches fiction writing at Hunter College in New York, and spends summers in Wellfleet.

JAMIE LEE MEADS

Jamie Lee Meads lives in Truro with her husband and infant daughter, and feels fortunate to be able to raise their child in such a wonderful place. Both her family and that of her husband have lived on the Outer Cape for many generations. She was 15 when she wrote the poem included in this anthology.

ANITA MEWHERTER

"I write poetry to find out who I am. It is cheaper than therapy," says Anita Mewherter. She is a member of the Wellfleet Writers' Guild and the Salt Wind Poets, and has had her poems published in the *Aurorean, CapeWomen, The Cape Codder* and *Prime Time.*

JUDITH PARTELOW

Judith Partelow is well-known to Cape Cod theatre-goers as an actor/director, but has also given poetry readings and been published in numerous small publications over the years. She lives in Harwich with her husband, Jeff Spencer, and works for the Healthcare Foundation of Cape Cod.

MARCIA PECK

Marcia Peck, a 'cellist with the Minnesota Orchestra, has been the recipient of artist fellowships from the Minnesota State Arts Board and Jerome Foundation, as well as residencies at Vermont Studio Center and Hambridge Center in Georgia. Her short story, "Abe," won the Castalia Bookmakers' 1989 Fiction Award and "An Unexpected Cadence" received Honorable Mention in the 1993 Tamarack Awards. Marcia and her husband Dave, and daughter Hadley, divide their summers between Orleans on Cape Cod and the Grand Teton Music Festival in Jackson, Wyoming.

CANDACE PERRY

Candace Perry's fiction includes plays as well as short stories. Her collection of short plays, *Lovers, Mothers & Others,* was recently produced by the Provincetown Theatre Company (PTC) and Narrowland Arts. She has also had short plays and a one-act produced by PTC, as well as a staged reading of her full-length play, *A Yellow Light.* She co-produced the Fall 2001 Outermost Radio Theatre for PTC and community radio WOMR. In addition to *CapeWomen,* her fiction has appeared in *Ms., The Sun, The Roanoke Review,* and *The Cape Cod Review.* She lives in Wellfleet where she is a clinical social worker and peace activist.

SUSAN POPE

Susan Pope has been writing and creating artwork since she was a child. She has an MFA in writing and has published two books: *Nan, Sarah and Clare: Letters Between Friends* and *Catching the Light.* She lives in Monument Beach on Cape Cod.

PAMELA CHATTERTON PURDY

Pamela Chatterton Purdy, born in New Canaan, CT, has been a longtime resident of Harwich Port on Cape Cod. An artist, teacher and diary keeper for much of her life and an adoptive parent, her book, *Beyond the Babylift: a Diary of an Adoption,* was published in 1987. "Sister Sally Loved to Death," published in this anthology, is an account from her diary of her sister's final days.

MARY ELLEN REDMOND
Mary Ellen Redmond was a member of the 2000 Cape Cod Poetry Slam Team and won first place in the 2001 *CapeWomen* Poetry Contest. Her work has appeared in *Dancing on Water, Divergent Voices, Lightening Strikes: Women, Transformation and Healing, The Cape Codder,* and *The Larcom.* She has lived on the Cape full time for the last eighteen years and currently resides in South Dennis.

VIRGINIA REISER
Virginia Reiser lives with her husband in the oldest house in Dennis. She has edited poetry and short story anthologies and her short fiction has been awarded prizes and fellowships, including first prize in the *CapeWomen* Annual Fiction Contest. Currently she is working on a novel, *The Soul Sits Alone.*

TESSA RUDD
Tessa Rudd was 14 years old and a student at the Lighthouse Charter School in Orleans when she wrote the poem published in this anthology. She graduated from Nauset High School in 2002 and is spending a post-graduate year at Northfield Mount Hermon School before attending college. She grew up in Provincetown and now lives in Eastham, where she is a lifeguard in the summer.

BETH SEISER
Beth Seiser grew up in Wellfleet, graduated from Hampshire College, and studied in China and Singapore as a Fulbright Scholar. She is now a freelance writer and the mother of two young boys. She lives in Eastham.

ROBIN SMITH-JOHNSON
Robin Smith-Johnson has had poems published in various journals including *CapeWomen, Sandscript, Voices International* and *Yankee Magazine.* Two of her poems were published recently in an anthology celebrating the child-parent bond, titled *Essential Love.* She lives in Mashpee with her family and works as the newsroom librarian at the *Cape Cod Times.*

BARBARA STEPHENS
Barbara Stephens teaches English and writing at Falmouth High School and Wheaton College. Her work has appeared in several journals and collections, including *Write from the Heart.* She earned her MFA in writing from Vermont College in 2001.

JADENE FELINA STEVENS
Jadene Felina Stevens is an award-winning poet who has been widely published, most recently in the April, 2002 issue of *Yankee Magazine.* She has been a three-time winner of the Phi Theta Kappa "Nota Bene Literary Awards," and received the PTK 1997 Citation Award. She is founder and Director of the Salt Winds Poets and recently led an eight-week workshop titled "Introduction to Poetry." She was co-editor for the Cape Cod Community College poetry anthology, *Dancing on Water* (2002), and editor for the anthology, *Village Poets of Sandwich.*

LINDA TURNER
Linda Turner lives in a funky old house in Brewster with her three inventive, creative and challenging teenagers. She began writing seriously almost immediately after learning how to hold a pen and now writes poetry because it is short. She has been published in various

anthologies, magazines and newspapers over the past 30 years and hopes someday to have a book in print that she doesn't have to publish herself. Meanwhile, she is gratified to have her work represented in this book.

THELMA TURNER

Thelma Turner of Harwich Port received her Doctor of Arts degree from SUNY, Albany, after writing a collection of short stories for her dissertation. Her writing experience includes articles for *The Cape Codder*, a short biography of Raoul Wallenberg, poems published in *The Aurorean*, and an ongoing writing practice in different genres. "All my life, I have had a love affair with words that has finally climaxed, for better or for worse, into a marriage," she says.

LAUREN WOLK

Lauren Wolk teaches writing and literature at Sturgis Charter School in Hyannis. Her first novel, *Those Who Favor Fire*, was published by Random House in 1999. She recently finished her second novel, *The Chameleon's Dish*, and is currently at work on her third. She lives in Centerville with her family.

In Memoriam

NANCY DINGMAN WATSON (1934–2001)

Longtime Truro resident Nancy ("Ding") Dingman Watson was an active and well-known member of the Outer Cape arts community. She was the author of more than 24 children's books and an award-winning children's musical, "Princess!"

She was twice a finalist in the Allen Ginsburg Poetry Competition, and more of her poetry can be found in published collections from Alan Dugan's workshops at the Truro Center for the Arts at Castle Hill in Truro. Four of her short plays were staged by the Provincetown Theatre Company, and in June of 2001 she was one of 60 new playwrights chosen to participate in the Ninth Annual Last Frontier Festival in Valdez, Alaska. She died in a car accident on June 28th, 2001, the day after returning home to Truro.

RACHEL ELLIS KAUFMAN (1912–2000)

Rachel Ellis Kaufman was born in Detroit, Michigan, on August 13, 1912. Both her parents were from the same region of Cape Cod and every summer of her childhood was spent at the family home, Orchardside, in East Sandwich. During her maturing years she studied art in New York at the Grand Central School of Fine Arts and The Applied School of Design. Throughout her busy life, which also included marriage, children, and extensive travels, Rachel always managed to keep painting, exhibiting, teaching, and writing poetry. In 1997 she returned to Cape Cod, the place she deemed her "spiritual home," where she spent her remaining years happily creating up to the day she died, March 13, 2000. The last word she spoke was a color, "Yellow."

ELINOR A. GELSEY (1933-2001)

Elinor A. Gelsey held a bachelor's degree in French from Wells College and a master's degree in psychology from the University of Houston. Her careers included magazine editor, psychologist, homemaker, and poet. She was a co-founder of the Chatham Old Village Association, and served as its president and vice president. More of her poetry can be seen at the website www.hometown.aol.com/elinoragelsey.

CONTRIBUTING ARTISTS

We wish to thank the following artists for generously
allowing us to use their work to illustrate this book:

Karri Ann Allrich
Rose Basile
Connie Black
Heather Blume
Barbara Cohen
Lois Edwina Grayson
Karen Gunderson
Diane Johnson
Joyce Johnson
Karen Klein
Kely Knowles
Coco Larrain
Linda McCausland
Barbara Melcher
Jeannie Motherwell
Liz Perry
Francie Randolph
Marian Roth
Rhoda M. Staley
Amy Szep
Sabina Teichman
Edith Vonnegut
Karen North Wells